Learning Puppet for
Windows Server

Organize your Windows environment using Puppet
tools to unload administrative burdens in a short time

Fuat Ulugay

PUBLISHING

BIRMINGHAM - MUMBAI

Learning Puppet for Windows Server

First published: August 2015

Production reference: 1170815

Published by Packt Publishing Ltd.
Livery Place
35 Livery Street
Birmingham B3 2PB, UK.

ISBN 978-1-78528-187-7

www.packtpub.com

Credits

Author
Fuat Ulugay

Reviewers
Rudi Broekhuizen

Jordan Olshevski

Commissioning Editor
Nadeem N. Bagban

Acquisition Editor
Harsha Bharwani

Content Development Editor
Dharmesh Parmar

Technical Editor
Tanmayee Patil

Copy Editor
Kausambhi Majumdar

Project Coordinator
Vijay Kushlani

Proofreader
Safis Editing

Indexer
Rekha Nair

Production Coordinator
Melwyn D'sa

Cover Work
Melwyn D'sa

About the Author

Fuat Ulugay is currently the IT and ERP director for SOCAR Turkey. He lives in Istanbul, Turkey. Also, he has worked as an SAP ABAP and SAP CRM consultant for more than 10 years.

He is a great fan of open source projects. He implements and teaches them whenever possible. He is good at penetration testing, network security monitoring, industrial control systems security, system administration, and virtualization. Also, he is leading and teaching the security team at his company. He has a blog at `http:/hacktr.org`, where he writes on open source and security-related topics.

I would like to thank my wife, Cigdem, for her continuous support while writing this book. Also, I would like to thank my little son, Omer Faruk, for his patience and playtime sacrifice when I was working on this book.

About the Reviewers

Rudi Broekhuizen is a system administrator at Naturalis Biodiversity Center in the Netherlands. From 2005 to 2013, his main focus was on Microsoft products, VMware virtualization, and networking.

Since 2013, he has been involved in transforming the IT organization to take a more DevOps-oriented approach. His main focus shifted to Linux, automated configuration management using Puppet, monitoring and analytics, OpenStack, and replacing closed source software with open source software.

To see what Rudi is currently working on, take a look at some of his code at `https://github.com/rudibroekhuizen` and `https://github.com/naturalis`.

Also, do not hesitate to leave a comment on his blog at `https://rudibroekhuizen.wordpress.com/`.

Jordan Olshevski is a professional services engineer at Puppet Labs. He has a background in software engineering and systems administration. He frequently consults enterprise organizations and has a passion for improving the lives of engineers through DevOps tooling and Agile methodologies. In his spare time, he enjoys listening to jazz music and contributing to the open source community.

www.PacktPub.com

Support files, eBooks, discount offers, and more

For support files and downloads related to your book, please visit www.PacktPub.com.

Did you know that Packt offers eBook versions of every book published, with PDF and ePub files available? You can upgrade to the eBook version at www.PacktPub.com and as a print book customer, you are entitled to a discount on the eBook copy. Get in touch with us at service@packtpub.com for more details.

At www.PacktPub.com, you can also read a collection of free technical articles, sign up for a range of free newsletters and receive exclusive discounts and offers on Packt books and eBooks.

https://www2.packtpub.com/books/subscription/packtlib

Do you need instant solutions to your IT questions? PacktLib is Packt's online digital book library. Here, you can search, access, and read Packt's entire library of books.

Why subscribe?

- Fully searchable across every book published by Packt
- Copy and paste, print, and bookmark content
- On demand and accessible via a web browser

Free access for Packt account holders

If you have an account with Packt at www.PacktPub.com, you can use this to access PacktLib today and view 9 entirely free books. Simply use your login credentials for immediate access.

Instant updates on new Packt books

Get notified! Find out when new books are published by following @PacktEnterprise on Twitter or the *Packt Enterprise* Facebook page.

Table of Contents

Preface

Puppet is a configuration management tool. It allows you to automate all your IT configurations by giving you the control of what you do to each node (Puppet agent), and also, focusing on when and how you do the configurations. In this context, Puppet is a cross-platform tool that is widely used for Unix-like and Microsoft Windows systems. However, it has been popularly used for Unix-like systems. This book provides insights into using Puppet for Windows administration tasks, such as server setup, application updates, and service management.

This book kicks off with the fundamentals of Puppet by helping you with the installation of Puppet on a Windows Server, and progresses with the introduction of the Foreman interface to manage Puppet nodes. Next, you will deal with the installation of Puppet agents on multiple clients and how to connect them to your Puppet server by grouping your nodes for easy management. Then, you will become familiar with the scripting of Puppet manifests along with an understanding of the module structure in Puppet. You will further move on to the installation of the Puppet Forge modules and their usage in Windows along with advanced topics such as facts, functions, and templates.

Moreover, you will venture into the security aspects for Windows by gaining insights into the various security settings that will make your server and clients more secure from hackers that use different attack vectors. You will also use Puppet and Chocolatey to install and update software.

Finally, you will round off by learning how to check the details of reporting and status monitoring along with the automation of installing and updating software for multiple Windows clients, arming you with ample artillery to tame Puppet for your future projects.

What this book covers

Chapter 1, Installing Puppet Server and Foreman, starts with an introduction to Puppet. It continues with the installation of the operating system of the server. Next, it deals with the installation of Puppet Server and Foreman. Finally, this chapter ends with the security settings of the server.

In this chapter, we start by learning what Puppet is. Then, we continue with the differences of Puppet implementation. We get hands-on experience by installing Puppet Server and Foreman. The last step is to learn how to keep your server secure. In the next chapter, we will deal with the Puppet agents and their installation on the hosts.

Chapter 2, Installing Puppet Agents, starts with setting up agents for single hosts. Next, it continues with modifying the MSI package for Puppet agent installation. After modifying the MSI file, this chapter shows how to use it to install the Puppet agents on multiple hosts by a third-party software and domain group policy. Lastly, the chapter finishes with the management of host certificates and host groups.

Chapter 3, Your First Modules, starts with writing your first module and continues with some basic module examples for file, directory, service, and user management. It also shows how to import the classes to Foreman and assign them to the hosts or host groups.

Chapter 4, Puppet Forge Modules for Windows, takes us into the world of Puppet Forge, where you can find many ready-to-use modules for Windows. The modules that are explained are registry, ACL, firewall, and reboot.

Chapter 5, Puppet Facts, Functions, and Templates, explains how to write Puppet facts, functions, and templates. This chapter shows how to display facts and write your custom facts. Also, it explains the templates to create dynamic content files. It gives details of the stdlib functions and how to create a custom function.

Chapter 6, Using Puppet for Windows Security, shows practices to make Windows more secure using Puppet. The purpose of this chapter is to make hacking activity harder for hackers and keep our systems as secure as possible. The sample practices are locking the startup folder and hosts file, starting the necessary services and stopping the unnecessary ones, setting the firewall rules, and finally, making the local administrator passwords unique.

Chapter 7, Reporting and Monitoring, shows many details about monitoring and checking the statuses of the host, such as how to see the statuses of the hosts in a summary, what information is available for the hosts, reporting the details of Foreman, and checking the definitions, statuses, and facts of the hosts in the terminal. Finally, this chapter deals with how to see the access and error logs for Foreman and Puppet.

Chapter 8, Installing Software and Updates, shows how to install a software using the Puppet package resource. Next, we continue with the details and usage of Chocolatey. Later, we use Puppet and Chocolatey together to make our installations and updates much easier. This chapter checks some of the commonly used software and how to always keep them updated. Finally, this chapter shows how to update the Puppet agents and uninstall the software.

What you need for this book

To learn and try the examples in this book, a computer with at least 8 GB of RAM and 100 GB of free hard disk space will be enough. You can use VMware or VirtualBox to install your server and test the clients. For system administrators, a server for Puppet, a domain controller, and some of the clients for testing will be enough.

Who this book is for

This book is for the Windows administrators who are looking for ways to automate the management tasks of Windows servers and clients. The target audience should have an experience in Windows administration and a basic knowledge of Linux and Puppet.

Conventions

In this book, you will find a number of styles of text that distinguish between different kinds of information. Here are some examples of these styles, and an explanation of their meaning.

Code words in text, database table names, folder names, filenames, file extensions, pathnames, dummy URLs, user input, and Twitter handles are shown as follows: "Use the ssh-keygen command to generate the keys."

A block of code is set as follows:

```
class firewallrules {
  windows_firewall::exception { 'WINRM':
    ensure       => present,
    direction    => 'in',
    action       => 'allow',
    enabled      => 'yes',
    protocol     => 'TCP',
    local_port   => '3389',
    remote_ip    => '10.10.10.20,10.10.10.21',
    display_name => 'Windows RDP Rule allow ips',
```

```
    description  => 'Inbound rule for Windows RDP allow [TCP
    3389]',
  }
}
```

Any command-line input or output is written as follows:

```
$ sudo puppet module install puppetlabs-reboot
```

New terms and **important words** are shown in bold. Words that you see on the screen, in menus or dialog boxes for example, appear in the text like this: "For the dashboard, from the **Monitor** menu click on **Dashboard**".

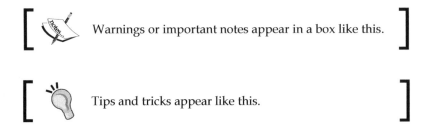

Warnings or important notes appear in a box like this.

Tips and tricks appear like this.

Reader feedback

Feedback from our readers is always welcome. Let us know what you think about this book—what you liked or may have disliked. Reader feedback is important for us to develop titles that you really get the most out of.

To send us general feedback, simply send an e-mail to feedback@packtpub.com, and mention the book title via the subject of your message.

If there is a topic that you have expertise in and you are interested in either writing or contributing to a book, see our author guide on www.packtpub.com/authors.

Customer support

Now that you are the proud owner of a Packt book, we have a number of things to help you to get the most from your purchase.

Downloading the example code

You can download the example code files from your account at http://www.packtpub.com for all the Packt Publishing books you have purchased. If you purchased this book elsewhere, you can visit http://www.packtpub.com/support and register to have the files e-mailed directly to you.

Downloading the color images of this book

We also provide you with a PDF file that has color images of the screenshots/diagrams used in this book. The color images will help you better understand the changes in the output. You can download this file from: `https://www.packtpub.com/sites/default/files/downloads/B04731_1877EN_Graphics.pdf`.

Errata

Although we have taken every care to ensure the accuracy of our content, mistakes do happen. If you find a mistake in one of our books—maybe a mistake in the text or the code—we would be grateful if you could report this to us. By doing so, you can save other readers from frustration and help us improve subsequent versions of this book. If you find any errata, please report them by visiting `http://www.packtpub.com/submit-errata`, selecting your book, clicking on the **Errata Submission Form** link, and entering the details of your errata. Once your errata are verified, your submission will be accepted and the errata will be uploaded to our website or added to any list of existing errata under the Errata section of that title.

To view the previously submitted errata, go to `https://www.packtpub.com/books/content/support` and enter the name of the book in the search field. The required information will appear under the **Errata** section.

Piracy

Piracy of copyright material on the Internet is an ongoing problem across all media. At Packt, we take the protection of our copyright and licenses very seriously. If you come across any illegal copies of our works, in any form, on the Internet, please provide us with the location address or website name immediately so that we can pursue a remedy.

Please contact us at `copyright@packtpub.com` with a link to the suspected pirated material.

We appreciate your help in protecting our authors, and our ability to bring you valuable content.

Questions

You can contact us at `questions@packtpub.com` if you are having a problem with any aspect of the book, and we will do our best to address it.

1
Installing Puppet Server and Foreman

Puppet is a configuration management software that allows the defining and enforcing of the desired state across your nodes and keeps them in this desired state. Nodes are the clients and servers that are connected to and managed by Puppet. Puppet supports both Linux and Windows environments. Also, it is available both commercially and in open source. In this book, we will deal only with the open source version.

However, you may also want to use or give Puppet Enterprise a go, which is the commercial solution. There is a virtual appliance available to download on the Puppet website `https://puppetlabs.com/download-learning-vm`. You can download and test it. It supports up to ten nodes for free. Of course, using the commercial version is easier as it has complete support and additional functionalities. The problem with it is that, you need to pay for it and have a budget. Following are the additional advantages, if you want to check the Enterprise Puppet. For more details, please check out the URL `https://puppetlabs.com/puppet/commercial`.

- Event inspection
- Role-based access control
- Puppet Server reporting
- Puppet Enterprise installer
- Puppet Enterprise console
- Puppet Node Manager

While reading books based on Puppet, we come across one little problem: the books are all about managing Linux systems. There are almost no resources explaining the details about managing Windows servers and clients. Thus, it was a challenge for me to use Puppet in the Windows environment. While doing this, I had to deal with many problems and learn the hard way. In this book, I will make it much easier for you to use Puppet for Windows. By the end of this book, you will have a solid understanding of how to write manifests for Windows and deal with the configuration problems. There will be practical step-by-step examples to complete the tasks. However, we will not delve much into technical and theoretical discussions. The book will show you one easy way of doing it. However, this does not mean that this is the only way to do it.

For example, we will use the Foreman web interface with Apache to manage hosts. This does not mean that this is the only way. You can use Puppet without any server and you can distribute the manifests with Git. This is called the masterless mode. You can only implement this with Apache and handle all the manifests from the terminal. You can also use the enterprise version. These are the perfectly possible ways of using Puppet, but may require more effort or money. The list of ways mentioned here is not exhaustive and every implementation method has not been covered. I have tried many ways and different usages, and came to the conclusion that using Foreman with Puppet is one of the easiest ways to start. This maximizes the benefits and minimizes the effort. However, this is subjective and some people may feel more comfortable without the graphical interface, or may switch to the enterprise version.

The differences between using Puppet with Windows and with Linux

Here, I will tell you some basic differences and not deal with an exhaustive list of all the differences between Windows and Linux. When checking out Puppet and writing the manifests, you may realize that it is much easier with Linux but harder to complete the same tasks with Windows. Here are some examples:

- **File resource**: This manages the permissions, ownership, and contents of the files. Permission settings do not work as successfully for Windows, as it works for Linux; we will use ACL module for this purpose.

- **Package resource**: This manages the packages and software installation. For Windows, we cannot directly install a package and keep it updated as we do in Linux, because Window sit does not have a package manager such as aptitude or yum. First, we need to first find the installer and send it to the host to handle the installation.

- **Puppet agent updates**: These are not easy with packages and requires manual steps.
- **Firewall**: This has support for Linux, but not an official support for Windows Firewall. We need to write our own manifests, or we can find a solution from Puppet Forge.
- **Windows Task Scheduler**: This is not fully supported and has only rudimentary functionality.
- **Windows Server**: This has a very limited support.

This list may continue in this way. Thus, as we can see, the differences are not in favor of Windows. In this book, we will solve these types of problems and show you how to handle them in an easy way.

Installing Puppet Server

We will start with the installation of the operating system of the Puppet Server. From now on, the Puppet Server will be called Puppet Master. We will use the Ubuntu server 14.04 LTS. Some users may prefer Enterprise Linux such as Red Hat or CentOS. If you prefer another flavor of Linux, this is also fine. Following are the server requirements. The requirements are fine for 500 to 1000 nodes. These requirements will change according to the number of your nodes:

- Ubuntu Server 14.04 LTS
- At least 4 GB RAM
- At least 2 Core CPU
- At least 40 GB of hard disk space

You can download the Ubuntu Server 14.04 LTS ISO from http://www.ubuntu. com/download/server. Using **Long Term Support** (**LTS**) versions, ensure that you do not have to upgrade your server for a long time and that there will be few issues about upgrading the distribution. If you want to test it first locally on your computer, you can also download and install VirtualBox from https://www.virtualbox.org/ wiki/Downloads. All the examples in this book have been created in VirtualBox.

You should have a new installation with the OpenSSH server. We will use SSH to connect to the server.

Connecting your server with SSH

We will use SSH to connect to our server. The installation is very easy. You can use the following command to install:

```
$ sudo apt-get install ssh -y
```

- `sudo`: This enables you to run a command with root privileges.
- `apt-get`: The APT package handling utility is used to install and uninstall software.
- `install`: This option is used with `apt-get` to install a package.
- `ssh`: This is the `ssh` server package name that will be installed.
- `-y`: The `apt-get` installation asks, "Do you want to continue [Y/n]?". This flag gives the answer as yes and the command runs without interruption.

If you use Windows as your operating system, you can connect using PuTTY. Download this from the link `http://www.chiark.greenend.org.uk/~sgtatham/putty/download.html`.

If you use Linux, you can connect from the terminal by the `ssh` command. For example,

```
$ sshusername@serverip
```

From now on, we will use `ssh` to connect to our server.

Installing Puppet

Puppet installation usually follows the following steps:

- Set the hostname
- Set FQDN
- Set the static IP, gateway and DNS
- Add the Puppet repositories
- Install Puppet

Let's have a look at each of them.

Setting the hostname

I will use `puppetmaster` as the hostname. You can use either `vim` or `nano` for text editing. If you have never used `vim` before, it will be easier for you to use `nano`.

```
$ sudonano /etc/hostname
```

- `sudo`: For configuration changes, we will need the root privileges. If we do not run the command with `sudo`, we cannot save our changes to the configuration file.
- `nano`: This is the command to run the nano text editor.
- `/etc/hostname`: This is the filename for the hostname configuration.

Use *CTRL* + *X* and *Y* to save.

Setting FQDN

I will use `puppetmaster.example.com`. Use the following command to edit the `/etc/hosts` file:

```
$ sudonano /etc/hosts
```

Change the contents as follows. Use your own IP according to your network.

```
127.0.0.1          localhost
127.0.1.1          puppetmaster.example.com
10.10.10.10        puppetmaster.example.com puppetmaster
```

To verify that the changes are effective, use the `hostname` and `hostname -f` commands.

```
puppet@puppetmaster:~$ hostname
puppetmaster
puppet@puppetmaster:~$ hostname -f
puppetmaster.example.com
puppet@puppetmaster:~$
```

 You also need to add the IP and **fully qualified domain name** (**FQDN**) to your company DNS, so that the other computers can find your server. I assume that, as a Windows system administrator, you already know how to do this. The IPs used here may not suit your network and IP ranges, so please change all the IP details throughout the book according to your needs.

Setting static IP, gateway, and DNS

For your server, give a static IP and define your gateway and nameserver IPs.

First, define your IP gateway and subnet mask. For this, we will edit the `/etc/network/interfaces` file. Following is the sample detail I have added for my Puppet Master:

```
$ sudonano /etc/network/interfaces
```

As you can see, the details are self-explanatory:

- eth0: This is the network interface name
- address: This is your server's IP
- netmask: This is the subnetmask
- broadcast: This is the broadcast IP
- gateway: This is the gateway IP

Now, let's set the nameserver IPs. To set NS records, we need to edit /etc/resolvconf/resolv.conf.d/base, as follows:

```
$ nano /etc/resolvconf/resolv.conf.d/base
```

The sample contents of this file are shown in the following screenshot. In our example, we are using the Google DNS IPs. Here, you can use your company's DNS IPs.

Downloading the example code

You can download the example code files from your account at http://www.packtpub.com for all the Packt Publishing books you have purchased. If you purchased this book elsewhere, you can visit http://www.packtpub.com/support and register to have the files e-mailed directly to you.

After saving the file, reboot the server. After rebooting, you can check using the following command whether you have the correct IP, netmask, and broadcast:

$ ifconfig

- `ifconfig`: This command is used to get info and make the changes in the network interfaces
- `eth0`: This is the network interface name
- `inet addr:10.10.10.10`: This is the IP address of our server
- `Bcast:10.10.10.255`: This is the broadcast IP
- `Mask:255.255.255.0`: This is the netmask IP

```
puppet@puppetmaster:~$ ifconfig
eth0      Link encap:Ethernet  HWaddr 08:00:27:67:57:d4
          inet addr:10.10.10.10  Bcast:10.10.10.255  Mask:255.255.255.0
          inet6 addr: fe80::a00:27ff:fe67:57d4/64 Scope:Link
          UP BROADCAST RUNNING MULTICAST  MTU:1500  Metric:1
          RX packets:305 errors:0 dropped:0 overruns:0 frame:0
          TX packets:320 errors:0 dropped:0 overruns:0 carrier:0
          collisions:0 txqueuelen:1000
          RX bytes:26804 (26.8 KB)  TX bytes:73202 (73.2 KB)

lo        Link encap:Local Loopback
          inet addr:127.0.0.1  Mask:255.0.0.0
          inet6 addr: ::1/128 Scope:Host
          UP LOOPBACK RUNNING  MTU:65536  Metric:1
          RX packets:467 errors:0 dropped:0 overruns:0 frame:0
          TX packets:467 errors:0 dropped:0 overruns:0 carrier:0
          collisions:0 txqueuelen:0
          RX bytes:345857 (345.8 KB)  TX bytes:345857 (345.8 KB)

puppet@puppetmaster:~$
```

Check whether the gateway is correct using the following command:

$ route -n

- `route`: This command shows and manipulates the IP routing table
- `-n`: This flag is to show the address details in numeric format instead of hostnames

```
puppet@puppetmaster:~$ route -n
Kernel IP routing table
Destination     Gateway         Genmask         Flags Metric Ref    Use Iface
0.0.0.0         10.10.10.1      0.0.0.0         UG    0      0        0 eth0
10.10.10.0      0.0.0.0         255.255.255.0   U     0      0        0 eth0
puppet@puppetmaster:~$
```

Lastly, check whether nameserver works correctly. Run the `nslookup` command and enter any address, as follows:

```
$ nslookup
```

- `nslookup`: This is the command to interactively query the Internet names servers. If no nameserver is provided, this will use the default one.

- `google.com`: When we enter any hostname, this will provide the details about it

- `exit`: This command ends `nslookup`

```
puppet@puppetmaster:~$ nslookup
> google.com
Server:         8.8.8.8
Address:        8.8.8.8#53

Non-authoritative answer:
Name:   google.com
Address: 216.58.208.110
> exit

puppet@puppetmaster:~$ ▊
```

As you can see in the preceding screenshot, it checks from `8.8.8.8`. Now we can say that our network settings are correct. To exit `nslookup`, you can use the `exit` command.

Adding the Puppet repositories

We will first add the Puppet repositories for installation. Secondly, we will update the repositories. Lastly, we will update our server before installing Puppet.

Here are the details to add the Puppet repositories:

```
$ sudowget https://apt.puppetlabs.com/puppetlabs-release-trusty.deb
$ sudodpkg -ipuppetlabs-release-trusty.deb
```

- `wget`: This is a utility for non-interactive downloads of files from the Web. We use this here to download the `puppetlabs-release-trusty.deb file`.

- `dpkg`: This is the package manager for Linux Debian. The option `-i` is used for installation.

Now, update the repository info, as follows:

```
$ sudo apt-get update
```

Lastly, install the updates, as follows:

```
$ sudo apt-get upgrade -y
```

- update: This option is used to resynchronize the package index files from their resources
- upgrade: This option is used to upgrade to the newest version of the already installed software

Installing Puppet

Now, it is time to install Puppet Master and its agent on your server. We will also do some configurations. The command to install Puppet is as follows:

```
$ sudo apt-get install -y puppetmaster puppet
```

Now, let's make sure that Puppet Master starts automatically. For this purpose, we need to edit /etc/default/puppetmaster. You need to change the START=no value to START=yes. If it is already yes, you can leave this as it is and continue. You also need to enable puppet agent on the server. We will edit the /etc/default/puppet file. Again, we need to make sure that START=yes exists. We also need to change the server details for the puppet agent. Change the /etc/puppet/puppet.conf file and enter the server details. Just after [main], add the line server=puppetmaster. example.com.

```
 GNU nano 2.2.6              File: /etc/puppet/puppet.conf

### File managed with puppet ###
## Module:            'puppet'

[main]
    server=puppetmaster.example.com
    # The Puppet log directory.
    # The default value is '$vardir/log'.
    logdir = /var/log/puppet

    # Where Puppet PID files are kept.
    # The default value is '$vardir/run'.
    rundir = /var/run/puppet

    # Where SSL certificates are kept.
    # The default value is '$confdir/ssl'.
    ssldir = $vardir/ssl

    # Allow services in the 'puppet' group to access key (Foreman + proxy)
    privatekeydir = $ssldir/private_keys { group = service }
    hostprivkey = $privatekeydir/$certname.pem { mode = 640 }

                          [ Read 75 lines ]
^G Get Help   ^O WriteOut   ^R Read File  ^Y Prev Page  ^K Cut Text   ^C Cur Pos
^X Exit       ^J Justify    ^W Where Is   ^V Next Page  ^U UnCut Text ^T To Spell
```

After making the changes, we will restart the services as shown here:

```
$ sudo service puppetmaster restart
$ sudo service puppet restart
```

Check whether they are running using the following commands:

```
$ sudo service puppetmaster status
$ sudo service puppet status
```

```
puppet@puppetmaster:~$ sudo service puppet restart
 * Restarting puppet agent                              [ OK ]
puppet@puppetmaster:~$ sudo service puppetmaster restart
 * Restarting puppet master                             [ OK ]
puppet@puppetmaster:~$ sudo service puppet status
 * agent is running
puppet@puppetmaster:~$ sudo service puppetmaster status
 * master is running
puppet@puppetmaster:~$
```

As you can see in the preceding screenshot, the services are running without any problem. So we completed the installation of Puppet Master and Puppet agent on our server.

Installing Foreman

After installing Puppet Master, our next step is to install the Foreman web user interface that will be used to manage and report. Foreman is an open source project that can be used with Puppet or Chef. With Foreman and Puppet, you can manage your servers for configuration management, orchestration, and monitoring. For installation of Foreman, we will first add the relevant repositories, and after that install it.

Add repository details, as follows:

```
$ sudo -i
# echo "deb http://deb.theforeman.org/ trusty stable" > /etc/apt/sources.
list.d/foreman.list
# echo "deb http://deb.theforeman.org/ plugins stable" >> /etc/apt/
sources.list.d/foreman.list
```

You can also use `sudonano` to add the details to the relevant files. In the preceding commands, `echo` outputs the text to the screen or a file. `>` overwrites the file, if it exists; if it does not exist, the file will be created. `>>` adds content to the end of the file without overwriting it.

We need to add the key for the repository, as we are manually adding the source details using this command:

```
# wget -q http://deb.theforeman.org/pubkey.gpg -O- | apt-key add -
```

Now we have successfully added the repository details; we can continue with the repository updates, as follows:

```
# apt-get update
```

We need Apache as our web server. So, we install apache2 and `foreman-installer` as shown in the following:

```
# apt-get install -y foreman-installer
```

The final step is to run the `foreman-installer`. It will take some time to complete. For my server, it took more than five minutes.

```
# foreman-installer
```

```
Installing          Info: RESOURCE Foreman_config_entry[db_pending_mig [99%]
Installing          Notice: /Stage[main]/Foreman::Database/Foreman::Ra [99%]
Installing          Notice: /Stage[main]/Foreman::Database/Foreman_con [99%]
Installing          Notice: /Stage[main]/Foreman::Database/Foreman::Ra [99%]
Installing          Info: RESOURCE Service[httpd]                       [99%]
Installing          Debug: Executing '/etc/init.d/apache2 stop'         [99%]
Installing          Debug: Executing '/etc/init.d/apache2 start'        [99%]
Installing          Notice: /Stage[main]/Apache::Service/Service[httpd  [99%]
Installing          Notice: /Stage[main]/Foreman::Database/Foreman::Ra [99%]
Installing          Debug: Executing '/usr/bin/apt-get -q -y -o DPkg::  [99%]
Installing          Notice: /Stage[main]/Foreman::Plugin::Bootdisk/For [99%]
Installing          Debug: Executing '/usr/bin/apt-get -q -y -o DPkg::  [99%]
Installing          Notice: /Stage[main]/Foreman::Plugin::Setup/Forema [99%]
Installing          Debug: Executing '/usr/sbin/update-rc.d foreman di [99%]
Installing          Notice: /Stage[main]/Foreman::Service/Service[fore [99%]
Installing          Debug: /Stage[main]/Foreman::Service/Service[forem [99%]
Installing          Notice: /Stage[main]/Foreman::Service/Exec[restart [99%]
Installing          Notice: /Stage[main]/Foreman_proxy::Register/Forem [99%]
Installing          Notice: /Stage[main]/Foreman_proxy::Register/Forem [99%]
Installing          Debug: Using settings: adding file resource 'rrddi [99%]
Installing          Done                                               [100%]
Installing          Done                                               [100%]
 []
  Success!
   * Foreman is running at https://puppetmaster.example.com
        Initial credentials are admin / rd5NMAYaz6SNovep
   * Foreman Proxy is running at https://puppetmaster.example.com:8443
   * Puppetmaster is running at port 8140
   The full log is at /var/log/foreman-installer/foreman-installer.log
root@puppetmaster:/mnt/cdrom#  _
```

Do not forget to write down the user and password details to connect your server. In the next section, we will see the basics of the user interface.

The Foreman interface

Now, just open a browser and enter your URL. In our example, the URL is `https://puppetmaster.example.com`. You will get the login page.

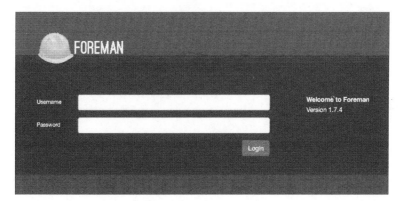

Log in with your username and password and you will get a screen as follows. In this screen, you will see only one host, which is our Puppet Master server. We added its agent before, and now we can see that it was connected just two minutes ago. This means that we can even manage Puppet Master with Puppet.

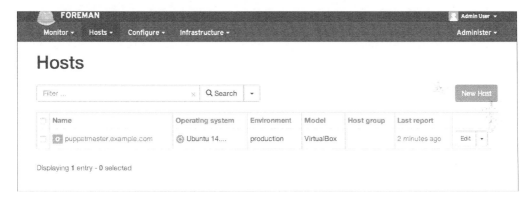

The next step is to change your password. From the right upper corner, go over to **Admin User** and click on **My account**. Set a new password as per your convenience. Make sure that the password is strong.

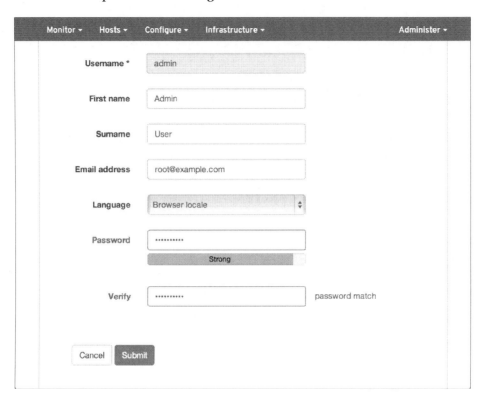

Now let's check out the dashboard. For the dashboard, from the **Monitor** menu click on **Dashboard**. In the dashboard, you will see the summary statuses of all your hosts. At the moment as we have only one host, there is not much detail. When we will have more hosts, we will check again, and then find that there will be many different statuses. Most of the statuses of your hosts will fall under one of the statuses listed, as follows:

- Hosts that have modifications without any error
- Hosts with errors

- Hosts with good reports in the last 35 minutes
- Out-of-sync hosts

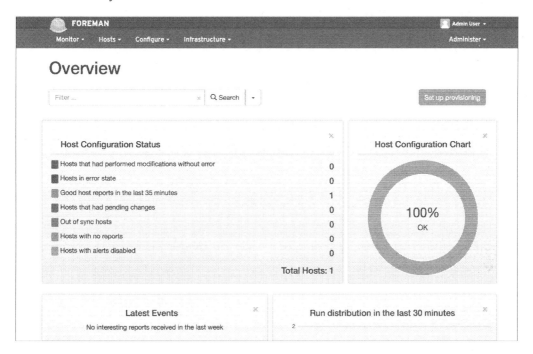

We will finish reviewing the Foreman interface. This will be enough for now. We will later see more details of the interface to manage our hosts.

Keeping your server secure

Puppet Master must be protected well. It is a high-risk asset. With Puppet, you can install software on all your servers and clients. Puppet agents on Linux and Windows run with root and admin rights respectively. Think about a scenario where a hacker gets control of it. He can easily run any command, install backdoors, and fully compromise your IT infrastructure.

I suggest using the Ubuntu Server version that does not have a graphical user interface. This will ensure that there will not be much unnecessary software on your Puppet Master. Having only the necessary software on it helps you to have a more secure server, and also to keep the performance higher.

Security rule:

Do not install any software that is not necessary. If vulnerable software does not exist, it cannot be attacked.

Backups

Keep frequent backups of your server.

There are many good backup solutions such as Backup Exec and Veeam. There are also hardware level backup solutions for storage devices. As a last option, you can also use free backup solutions such as Burp backup or a **version control system** (**VCS**). VCS will only back up your code and configuration.

Backup solutions and how to handle them is out of the scope of the book. Every company and system administrator has or should have their backup solution. If you do not have one, it is really time to implement one of the solutions as soon as possible. Without backups, your most important concern and risk will be business continuity.

Keeping your server up to date

Every day we see that there are new vulnerabilities, and with new security updates they are patched. So you must have a good policy of updates. The updates are very easy with Ubuntu; you only run two commands, as follows:

```
$ sudo apt-get update
$ sudo apt-get upgrade
```

I will not explain these commands again. You can check the section *Installing Puppet* in this chapter to see the details if you need.

Before updating your server, ensure that in case of problems, you can go back. If you are using a virtual machine, such as Puppet Master, take a snapshot before the updates. If you use hardware, take a new backup before you start.

Lastly, it is also a good idea to have a development environment. Testing the updates in development and then updating the production server would be a good practice.

Do not enable root account

Some administrators do not feel happy about entering a `sudo` command and password whenever there is a need for root privilege. To simply bypass this problem, they enable the root account and use it for every task.

The problem with using the root account is that, you have many processes and software running with root privileges. Assuming that one of them is vulnerable, and a hacker targets your server. When the hacker uses this vulnerability and opens a shell, the privileges that he will have are directly related to the process. So, if the process runs with root privileges, the hacker gains root access. Root access implies total control of the server. If the process is using a limited user account, the hacker will gain these privileges. This means that he still has a long way to go and find some way to escalate the privileges.

Also, when you use the root account, you also need to protect the server from yourself. The root account can do everything; with great power comes great responsibility. If you do something wrong, accidentally, you may need to restore your server from a backup. If you do not have a backup, things may get worse.

Always use a limited account and use `sudo` only when needed. This will protect you from hackers and also from yourself.

Check status of the root account, as follows:

```
$ sudopasswd root -S
```

If not locked, lock it using the following:

```
$ sudopasswd root -l
```

> From now on, in this chapter, all the following details are not related to the implementation and installation of Puppet. However, it is suggested to complete these steps in a live environment. When learning in a test environment, security may not be your initial concern. In this case, simply go to *Chapter 2, Installing Puppet Agents*

The user password policy

Another important point is to have a decent password policy. With the correct password policy, we will make it harder for the passwords to be cracked. In the Windows Group Policy, there are also settings for password policy. Thus, the Windows administrators can easily understand its necessity. Here are some points to improve upon.

Do not use old passwords that have been used before

To limit the old passwords that can be used, we need to edit the /etc/pam.d/ common-password file. **PAM is Pluggable Authentication Modules**. PAM enables us to change the authentication process of Linux.

```
$ sudonano /etc/pam.d/common-password
```

```
password    [success=1 default=ignore]    pam_unix.so obscure sha512
remember=5
```

- pam_unix.so is the default PAM module
- obscure sha512 will encrypt the new passwords with sha512
- success=1 skips the next rule
- remember=5 will prevent the user from using the last five passwords

Using at least a 10 char complex password

To set more complex passwords, we will install the libpam-cracklib library, as follows:

```
$ sudo apt-get install libpam-cracklib
```

After this, we again edit the /etc/pam.d/common-password file as follows:

```
$ sudonano/etc/pam.d/common-password
```

```
password  requisite  pam_cracklib.so retry=3 minlen=10 difok=3 ucredit=-1
lcredit=-1 dcredit=-1 ocredit=-1
```

- retry=3 ensures that while setting the password, if the user cannot successfully set a password three times, the passwd command will abort
- minlen=10 is the minimum length for the password

- `difok=3` is the minimum number of characters that must be different from those of the previous password

- `ucredit=-1` sets the minimum number of required uppercase characters to 1

- `lcredit=-1` sets the minimum number of required lowercase characters to 1

- `dcredit=-1` sets the minimum number of required digits to 1

- `ocredit=-1` sets the minimum number of required symbols to 1

Here are the `/etc/pam.d/common-password` details after the changes:

```
# here are the per-package modules (the "Primary" block)
password        requisite               pam_cracklib.so retry=3 minlen=10 difok=3 ucredit=-1 lcredit=-1 dcredit=-1 ocredit=-1
password        [success=1 default=ignore]    pam_unix.so obscure use_authtok try_first_pass sha512 remember=5
# here's the fallback if no module succeeds
password        requisite               pam_deny.so
# prime the stack with a positive return value if there isn't one already;
# this avoids us returning an error just because nothing sets a success code
# since the modules above will each just jump around
password        required                pam_permit.so
# and here are more per-package modules (the "Additional" block)
# end of pam-auth-update config
~
```

Expiring password in 90 days

The password expiration details are in the `/etc/login.defs` file. Change the value of `PASS_MAX_DAYS` to `90` and it will be forced to update the password every 90 days, as follows:

`$ sudonano/etc/login.defs`

`PASS_MAX_DAYS    90`

Locking account

This policy makes sure that any brute force attempt will fail, or need too much time to complete. We will lock the user account for 10 minutes, if five times there are consecutive login failures. For this purpose, we need to modify the `/etc/pam.d/common-auth` file. After the lock and wait time, if the user successfully logs in with the correct password, the failed attempts counter will be reset to zero. Otherwise, each failed attempt after the lock will cause another 10 minutes of lock. So, I suggest here that you keep a backup user with the sudo rights, as follows:

`$ sudonano/etc/pam.d/common-auth`

`auth    required    pam_tally2.so deny=5 onerr=fail unlock_time=600`

- `pam_tally2.so` is the PAM module that comes with Ubuntu installation and used for account locks.

- `deny=5` is the setting used to set the number of failed logins to lock an account.

- `onerr=fail` if something weird happens, the PAM login status will be `fail` or `success`. The default status is `fail`.

- `unlock_time=600` is the number of seconds after which the account will be unlocked.

After completing all the changes, restart your server with the `reboot` command for all the changes to be applied. This is done as follows:

```
$ sudo reboot
```

You can check a user's login attempts with the following command:

```
$ sudo pam_tally2 -u username
```

- `pam_tally2` is the command for the login counter PAM
- `-u` is used to set the user

Here is an example output after two unsuccessful login attempts:

```
root@puppetmaster:~# pam_tally2 -u puppet2
Login           Failures Latest failure      From
puppet2             2      02/25/15 18:10:29  10.10.10.2
root@puppetmaster:~#
```

If you want to reset the counter and unlock the user, you can use the following command. `-r` switch is used to reset the failures counter.

```
$ sudo pam_tally2 -u username -r
```

Using SSH with key file to connect

This step makes sure that even if somebody gets your password, it will not be usable. Thus, we will use the SSH key files. The SSH key files are used to identify yourself to an SSH server using the public-key cryptography and challenge-response authentication. We will disable the password logon option and it will be only possible to connect with a key file. We will also put a password to the key file, to make sure that it is also not usable without the password.

Creating the public and private key

Use the `ssh-keygen` command to generate the keys, as follows:

```
$ ssh-keygen
```

```
puppet@puppetmaster:~$ ssh-keygen
Generating public/private rsa key pair.
Enter file in which to save the key (/home/puppet/.ssh/id_rsa):
Enter passphrase (empty for no passphrase):
Enter same passphrase again:
Your identification has been saved in /home/puppet/.ssh/id_rsa.
Your public key has been saved in /home/puppet/.ssh/id_rsa.pub.
The key fingerprint is:
b1:77:55:2a:08:9b:19:4f:cc:c7:c2:6a:ee:c1:c5:55 puppet@puppetmaster
The key's randomart image is:
+--[ RSA 2048]----+
|        o+.. .E .|
|        O=.+   o |
|        =oo+.  o |
|        ooo   o  |
|       +S.. .    |
|        +. .     |
|        . .      |
|         .       |
|                 |
+-----------------+
puppet@puppetmaster:~$ ▓
```

`ssh-keygen` first asks for the folder to save the keys. Just push the *Enter* key and continue. The next question is the passphrase. Make sure that you enter a password. Using the password with your key makes sure that, when somebody gets your key, it will be unusable.

Now go to the `.ssh` folder, as follows:

```
$ cd .ssh
```

Under this folder, you will see these two files:

- `id_rsa`: Private key
- `id_rsa.pub`: Public key

We need to add the details of the public key to a file called `authorized_keys`. This will make it possible to log in with the private key.

```
$ cat id_rsa.pub >authorized_keys
```

- The `cat` command displays the content of a file in the terminal
- The `>` symbol adds the content of a command output to a file and if the file has content, it will be overwritten
- The `authorized_keys` is the file that will be required for the `ssh` connection with a key

Here is an example screenshot:

```
puppet@puppetmaster:~$ cd .ssh/
puppet@puppetmaster:~/.ssh$ ls
id_rsa  id_rsa.pub
puppet@puppetmaster:~/.ssh$ cat id_rsa.pub
ssh-rsa AAAAB3NzaC1yc2EAAAADAQABAAABAQCrH40ZP8E0lxOu6e5sFFJSYjKyHSLP+ylO/nx1vGWv2d5LyOLGoXYinN5U5aYs6F4ADLJn1F
H6EJxw/5Mik6pa2AMBpLfGoy0h2Qs4oZYHOoUNRtZAQiyVM/khNHA2JXxE5h/b82RZmNHAsxSKYYpa6rkjPGl/J7Is7+0XtmEodeoagW05GKYY
QGxPM9at5IpOBipWuVV53ALpz948T0C8h053m83BFYRSZLDbi3Q7jLvKdRv/yQgO7SlicAfQGxeife5e5nQLcJ+iFh5fDhNHY8UoDkbPeDjb31
cE0oab6RPGOVENo6zwBmHDU1BQ1vPz7ARi6OkguuudEAr/TwTJ puppet@puppetmaster
puppet@puppetmaster:~/.ssh$ cat id_rsa.pub > authorized_keys
puppet@puppetmaster:~/.ssh$ ls -l
total 12
-rw-rw-r-- 1 puppet puppet  401 Feb 26 21:30 authorized_keys
-rw------- 1 puppet puppet 1766 Feb 26 21:28 id_rsa
-rw-r--r-- 1 puppet puppet  401 Feb 26 21:28 id_rsa.pub
puppet@puppetmaster:~/.ssh$
```

Change the authorized_keys file permissions, otherwise the key will not work. This is done as follows:

```
$ chmod 600 authorized_keys
```

This command will allow only the user to edit and write the file; any group or other users will not be able to change it.

Getting the key to your computer and converting it into the PuTTY format

Now, we need to get the contents of `id_rsa` to our computer that we will use to connect to Puppet Master.

To do this, you can use FileZilla to connect and download the file. Or you can use any FTP client with SFTP support. Here is a screenshot for the SFTP connection definition:

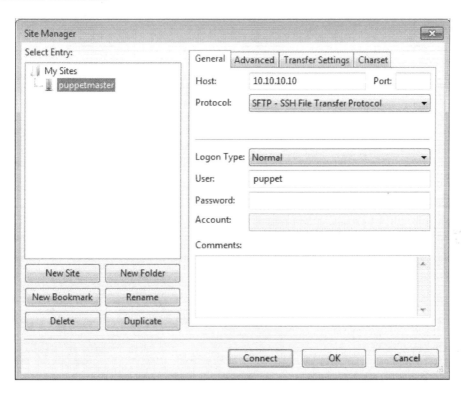

You need to enter the following:

- **Host**: The server IP is `10.10.10.10`. This is the IP that we gave to our Puppet Master server while installing.
- **Protocol**: SFTP.
- **Logon Type**: Normal.
- **User**: Your username.
- **Password**: Your password.

After you have filled the details, click the **Connect** button. When you connect, you will see your user folder and the .ssh folder, as follows:

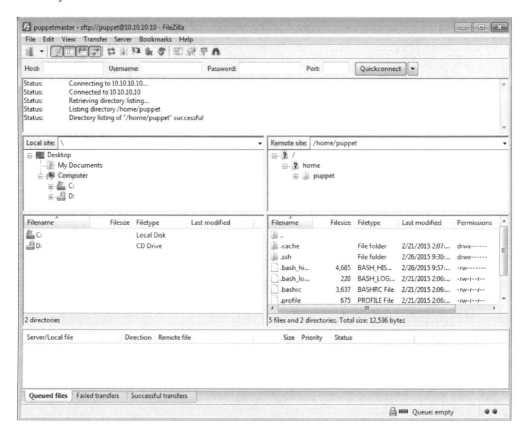

Download the id_rsa file to your documents folder. After this, you need to convert the file with PuTTYgen.exe. Open PuTTYgen.exe and click the **Load** button. You also need to select the **All Files (*.*)** option, as shown here:

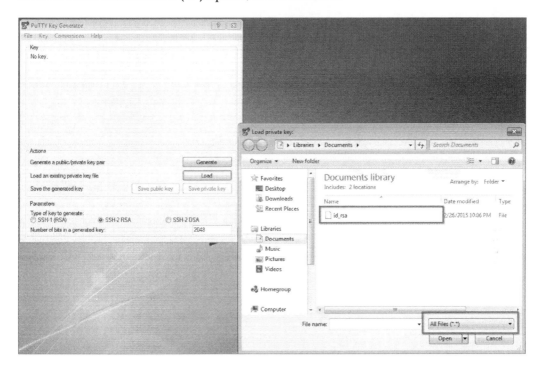

After you click it open, it will ask for the password. After this, click on **Save private key** and give a name to your key. I saved it as puppetmaster.ppk. Now, we are ready to use this key to connect to Puppet Master.

To do it, first fill in the details as follows:

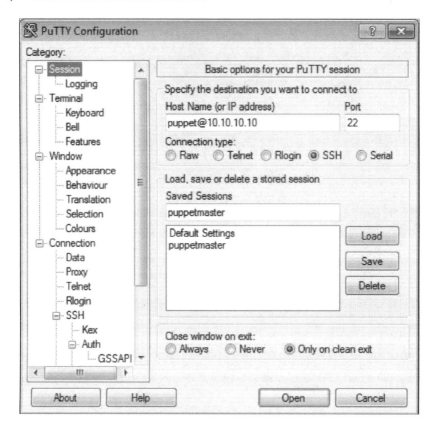

- **Host Name**: `username@ipaddress`
- **Port**: `22`
- **Saved Sessions**: Give a name for the session

Now go to **SSH | Auth**. Select the key file, as follows:

After this, go back to **Session** from the **Category** section and use the **Save** button. This will make sure that you can reuse the connection and do not have to define the same settings again.

Now you will be able to connect by double-clicking your saved session name. It will ask for the key file password and then you will be able to connect.

Connecting from Linux

To connect from Linux systems, you do not need to convert the private key. You can just connect from the terminal with the `ssh` command, as follows:

```
$ sshusername@serverip -ikeyfile
```

When I change this command to my example, it will be as shown here:

```
$ sshpuppet@10.10.10.10 -iid_rsa
```

Disabling the SSH logins with a password

This is our last step for SSH. After disabling the password login option, there will be no possibility for an hacker to use brute force against an account. Also, there will be no possibility to log in, even if the hacker knows the password.

We need to change the /etc/ssh/sshd_config file to disable password, as follows:

```
$ sudonano /etc/ssh/sshd_config
```

Find the PasswordAuthentication text, uncomment it, and set the value to no.

```
# To enable empty passwords, change to yes (NOT RECOMMENDED)
PermitEmptyPasswords no

# Change to yes to enable challenge-response passwords (beware issues with
# some PAM modules and threads)
ChallengeResponseAuthentication no

# Change to no to disable tunnelled clear text passwords
PasswordAuthentication no

# Kerberos options
```

After changing the value and saving the file, restart the ssh service, as shown here:

```
$ sudo service ssh restart
```

Now, here is the output when I try to log in without the key:

The firewall rules

For the servers and clients, the rule for security is: "Deny all incoming connections and allow only those needed." Here are the steps:

- Check which ports to keep open
- Define the firewall rules
- Make the firewall rules persistent

Checking which ports to keep open

We will use `netstat` to check the listening ports and running services. Here, we already know that for administrative purposes, we need to keep the SSH port 22 open. But we also need to check other ports that Puppet and Foreman are using. The command to check the listening ports and services is as follows:

```
$ sudonetstat -nlput
```

- `netstat`: The command to check network connections.
- n flag: This shows addresses in the numeric format
- l flag: This shows only the listening ports
- p flag: This shows the PID name of the program that the socket belongs to
- u flag: This shows the UDP ports
- t flag: This shows the TCP ports

```
puppet@puppetmaster:~$ sudo netstat -nlput
[sudo] password for puppet:
Active Internet connections (only servers)
Proto Recv-Q Send-Q Local Address           Foreign Address         State       PID/Program name
tcp        0      0 0.0.0.0:22              0.0.0.0:*               LISTEN      804/sshd
tcp        0      0 127.0.0.1:5432          0.0.0.0:*               LISTEN      891/postgres
tcp        0      0 0.0.0.0:8443            0.0.0.0:*               LISTEN      1024/ruby
tcp        0      0 127.0.0.1:40605         0.0.0.0:*               LISTEN      1673/foreman
tcp        0      0 127.0.0.1:43946         0.0.0.0:*               LISTEN      1531/rack
tcp6       0      0 :::80                   :::*                    LISTEN      1401/apache2
tcp6       0      0 :::22                   :::*                    LISTEN      804/sshd
tcp6       0      0 ::1:5432                :::*                    LISTEN      891/postgres
tcp6       0      0 :::443                  :::*                    LISTEN      1401/apache2
tcp6       0      0 :::8140                 :::*                    LISTEN      1401/apache2
udp6       0      0 :::69                   :::*                                832/in.tftpd
puppet@puppetmaster:~$
```

Here are the ports that we need to keep open:

- `22`: `ssh`
- `80,445`: HTTP and HTPPS ports to connect Foreman
- `8443`: Foreman proxy is running on this port as a proxy
- `8140`: Puppet Master listens to this port

You can also remember that in the section *Installing Foreman* when the installation finishes, it gives the details about the `8443` and `8140` ports.

Defining firewall rules

We will use iptables as the firewall. It comes preinstalled on the Ubuntu Server. First, let's check the rules that we have. If no rules are defined previously, all the policies will be in the `ACCEPT` state. The commands to check the iptables rules are as follows:

```
$ sudoiptables -L -v
```

- `iptables`: This is the command to manage the firewall
- `L` flag: This lists all rules
- `v` flag: Verbose output. This shows the rule options and packet counters

```
puppet@puppetmaster:~$ sudo iptables -L -v
Chain INPUT (policy ACCEPT 156 packets, 136K bytes)
 pkts bytes target     prot opt in     out     source               destination

Chain FORWARD (policy ACCEPT 0 packets, 0 bytes)
 pkts bytes target     prot opt in     out     source               destination

Chain OUTPUT (policy ACCEPT 150 packets, 137K bytes)
 pkts bytes target     prot opt in     out     source               destination
puppet@puppetmaster:~$
```

Allowing ingress traffic for the SSH port 22

We will accept traffic from any source when the destination port is port `22`. Here is the command:

```
$ sudoiptables -A INPUT -p tcp --dport 22 -j ACCEPT
```

- `-A` flag is used for adding rules.
- `-p tcp`, here `p` flag is for the protocol definition and TCP is the protocol.

- `--dport 22`, here, `dport` is the destination port definitions and the port is 22.
- `-j ACCEPT`, here, `j` flag tells what to do. Here, we accept the packet, if it matches the rule.

Allowing ingress traffic for HTTP port 80

We will accept traffic from any source when the destination port is port 80. Here is the command:

```
$ sudoiptables -A INPUT -p tcp --dport 80 -j ACCEPT
```

Allowing ingress traffic for HTTPS port 443

We will accept traffic from any source when the destination port is port 443. Here is the command:

```
$ sudoiptables -A INPUT -p tcp --dport 443 -j ACCEPT
```

Allowing ingress traffic for Foreman proxy port 8443

We will accept traffic from any source when the destination port is port 8443. Here is the command:

```
$ sudoiptables -A INPUT -p tcp --dport 8443 -j ACCEPT
```

Allowing ingress traffic for Puppetmaster port 8140

We will accept traffic from any source when the destination port is port 8140. Here is the command:

```
$ sudoiptables -A INPUT -p tcp --dport 8140 -j ACCEPT
```

Allowing all that is established from us

We need to define this rule. Otherwise, any traffic connection will not be complete. We will be able to send traffic outside, but never be able to get answers back. So, we will allow any incoming packet that is related to our outgoing traffic.

```
$ sudoiptables -A INPUT -m state --state ESTABLISHED,RELATED -j ACCEPT
```

- `-m`: This flag is used to match certain conditions. It can be used with different types of modules.
- `state --state ESTABLISHED,RELATED`: `state` is the module name that checks the statuses of a connection. Here, we allow any connection that is related to the established and related connections.

Denying all the incoming traffic

This time, we do not give any protocol or port number. So, this means that all the input traffic will be dropped.

```
$ sudoiptables -P INPUT DROP
```

After completing the rules, let's check the iptables rules again:

```
root@puppetmaster:~# iptables -L -v
Chain INPUT (policy ACCEPT 0 packets, 0 bytes)
 pkts bytes target     prot opt in     out     source               destination
  215 13928 ACCEPT     tcp  --  any    any     anywhere             anywhere             tcp dpt:ssh
    0     0 ACCEPT     tcp  --  any    any     anywhere             anywhere             tcp dpt:http
    0     0 ACCEPT     tcp  --  any    any     anywhere             anywhere             tcp dpt:https
    0     0 ACCEPT     tcp  --  any    any     anywhere             anywhere             tcp dpt:8443
    0     0 ACCEPT     tcp  --  any    any     anywhere             anywhere             tcp dpt:8140
    6   852 ACCEPT     all  --  any    any     anywhere             anywhere             state RELATED,ESTABLISHED
    0     0 DROP       all  --  any    any     anywhere             anywhere

Chain FORWARD (policy ACCEPT 0 packets, 0 bytes)
 pkts bytes target     prot opt in     out     source               destination

Chain OUTPUT (policy ACCEPT 45 packets, 5002 bytes)
 pkts bytes target     prot opt in     out     source               destination
root@puppetmaster:~#
```

As you can see in the preceding screenshot, all the rules are defined in the order that we defined.

IMPORTANT:

Define the "deny all" rule last. The order of the rules is important. The first rule will be applied first. So, if you first define the "deny all" rule, you will not be able to connect with SSH and your connection will drop.

Making the iptables rules persistent

The rules we defined are not persistent. So whenever you restart your server, the rules will be lost. To prevent this, we will install `iptables-persistent`. This software will keep our rules and will enable them at the startup. First install it using the following command:

```
$ sudoapt-get install iptables-persistent
```

While installing, it will ask you to save the current configuration to a file name such as `/etc/iptables/rules.v4`. Answer this with a yes. The second question will be about IPv6. We did not define any rules for it, so answer no for this.

After completing the setup, reboot your server and list the rules of iptables to see that they are still there.

Summary

In this chapter, we started by learning what Puppet is. After this, we continued with the differences between Puppet implementations. We got hands-on experience by installing Puppet Server and Foreman. The final step was learning about how to keep your server secure. In the next chapter, we will deal with the Puppet agents and their installation on the hosts.

2
Installing Puppet Agents

In the previous chapter, we completed the setup of our Puppet Master server. So far, this has been purely in Linux. From now on, we will mostly deal with Windows, Foreman GUI, and Puppet Master. In this chapter, we will learn how to:

- Install the Puppet agent
- Modify the installation file
- Use third-party software to install the Puppet agent on multiple hosts
- Use a domain controller to install Puppet on multiple agents

The first step is to install a Puppet agent on a host computer and make the necessary configurations, so that the host and server can have a connection.

Downloading and installing the Puppet agent

This is a very easy step. We just need to log in to one of our Windows servers or clients, and install the Puppet agent. You can download the latest installation file from `https://downloads.puppetlabs.com/windows/`. Always download the latest version that is compatible with your server. Make sure that the version number of your agent is not greater than your Puppet Master's version.

You can check your Puppet's version in Puppet Master using the following command:

```
$ puppet --version
```

Finally, download the correct version that is supported by your server/client, that is, 32 bits or 64 bits.

After the download, you need administrative rights to install the software. Just double-click and install the agent using the **Next**, **Install**, and, **Finish** buttons. You just need to enter the FQDN of the server correctly, as shown in the following screenshot:

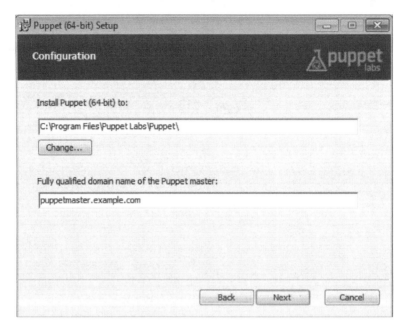

After the installation, we can check whether everything has proceeded fine. Normally, you do not need to check whether it was installed properly. However, you may need the following details for troubleshooting. So, it is best to learn how to deal with the agent, and then test whether it is running without any problems.

The Puppet agent runs as a Windows service. Let's check whether there is one such service. When we check it, we can see whether it is listed as a service and whether it has already started, as shown in the following screenshot:

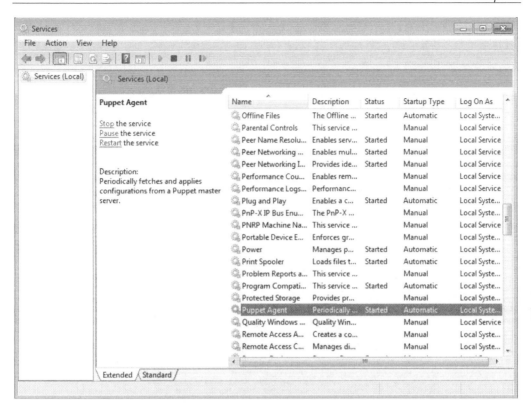

Now, from the Command Prompt, we will check the version of the agent and try a test run.

You will need to open `cmd.exe` with administrator rights, otherwise the Puppet test will work incorrectly. You will, also, need to run a new instance after the installation. If you try to use an already running Command Prompt, it will fail to find the `puppet` command, as the new path definitions are not active in the running instance.

The command for checking the version in Windows is also the same as that of Puppet Master. The command is as follows:

```
C:\> puppet --version
```

Test run the agent using the following command:

```
C:\> puppet agent --test
```

For puppet to correctly resolve puppetmaster.example.com, it is best to add a record in your DNS server. This detail was covered in *Chapter 1, Installing Puppet Server and Foreman*. If you did not add a record in your DNS, you can also change the hosts file locally using C:\Windows\System32\drivers\etc\hosts. However, this is not suggested because in this case, you have to manually modify each computer's hosts file.

In the following screenshot, we can see that the agent version is 3.7.4 and the test run gives a certificate error. This is normal. We will now sign the certificate from Foreman and after this, the agent will be able to connect. The agent version and the result of the test run is as shown here:

```
Administrator: C:\Windows\system32\cmd.exe

Microsoft Windows [Version 6.1.7600]
Copyright (c) 2009 Microsoft Corporation.    All rights reserved.

C:\Users\vagrant>puppet --version
3.7.4

C:\Users\vagrant>puppet agent --test
Exiting; no certificate found and waitforcert is disabled

C:\Users\vagrant>_
```

Signing the certificate

Go to the Foreman web user interface. From the menu, select **Infrastructure** | **Smart Proxies**. On the smart proxies screen, as shown in the following screenshot, select **Certificates**, as this is the section to manage your hosts' certificates:

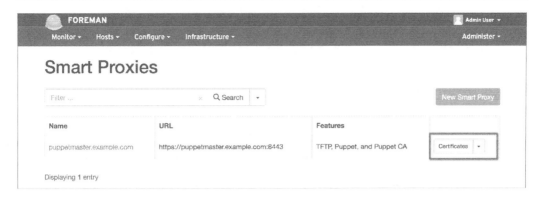

Here, you will see the new host and its status. As you can see in the following screenshot, the host is waiting in the **pending** status. Click the **Sign** button and sign the new host's certificate:

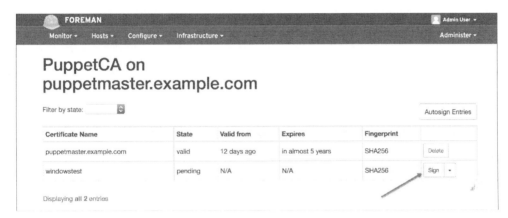

After this, we can go back to our host and run a new test to see what happens:

```
C:\Users\vagrant>puppet agent --test
Info: Caching certificate for windowstest
Info: Caching certificate_revocation_list for ca
Info: Caching certificate for windowstest
Warning: Unable to fetch my node definition, but the agent run will continue:
Warning: Error 400 on SERVER: Failed to find windowstest via exec: Execution of
'/etc/puppet/node.rb windowstest' returned 1:
Info: Retrieving pluginfacts
Info: Retrieving plugin
Info: Caching catalog for windowstest
Info: Applying configuration version '1425654995'
Info: Creating state file C:/ProgramData/PuppetLabs/puppet/var/state/state.yaml
Notice: Finished catalog run in 0.02 seconds

C:\Users\vagrant>puppet agent --test
Info: Retrieving pluginfacts
Info: Retrieving plugin
Info: Caching catalog for windowstest
Info: Applying configuration version '1425654995'
Notice: Finished catalog run in 0.02 seconds
```

During the first run, the host successfully connected to the server. However, there is an error informing that it cannot find the node definition. This is fine. In the first connection, the node definition will be created. As you can see in the preceding screenshot, when you run the test again, there is no error because the node definition was created previously.

Now, let's switch back to Foreman and check whether the host details can be seen here. From the menu, select **Hosts | All hosts**. The details are as follows. We can see that the new host is added to our hosts list:

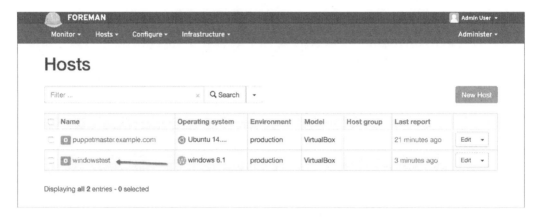

Summarizing, you only need the following two steps:

- Install the agent with correct server details
- Sign the certificate

All the other steps are for information and troubleshooting when you have problems of host connections.

Installing the Puppet agent on multiple clients

After looking at how to install the Puppet agent on one Windows host, it may occur to you that installing the agent on each host manually will be really cumbersome, if you have hundreds or thousands of hosts. In this section, we will deal with the different options of installing the agent on multiple hosts.

Here are some options, as follows:

- You can use third-party software
- You can use the domain controller
- You can use the Microsoft System Center Configuration Manager

Modifying the MSI file

As we are sticking to free tools to get things done, it is hard to find a software that is capable of modifying the MSI settings and sending the installation to multiple hosts. However, if you have a configured MSI file to use, it is reasonable to use a free or shareware software.

In this section, we will modify the Puppet agent installation MSI, so that it includes the FQDN server. After this, we can silently push the installation and it can run in the background without disturbing the users of the clients and servers.

To change the MSI file of the Puppet agent installation, we will use **Orca** from Microsoft. To get Orca, we need to install **Microsoft Windows SDK for Windows 7 and .NET Framework 4**. Go to `http://www.microsoft.com/en-us/download/details.aspx?id=8279` and download it. Before installing this SDK, you need to install .NET 4. If you do not have this, the link to download it is `http://www.microsoft.com/en-us/download/details.aspx?id=17851`.

After downloading the SDK, run the `winsdk_web.exe` file. Use the **Next** button, until you see the following screen. Just select **Tools** under **Windows Native Code Development** and continue the installation:

After the installation is complete, go to the `C:\Program Files\Microsoft SDKs\ Windows\v7.1\Bin` folder and find `Orca.msi`:

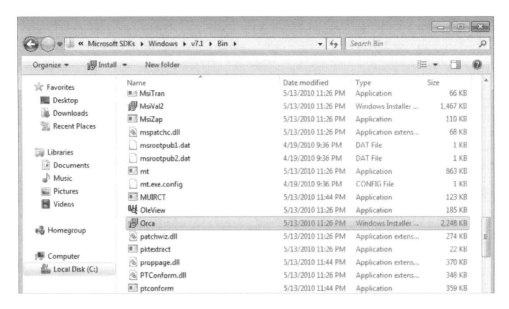

This is the software that we need, to change the MSI file details. Install this software. During installation, when asked, select the **Typical** installation. When the installation is complete, you will see the **Orca** link in the **Start** menu:

After executing Orca, open the Puppet agent installation MSI file. Select **CustomAction** on the left-hand side section:

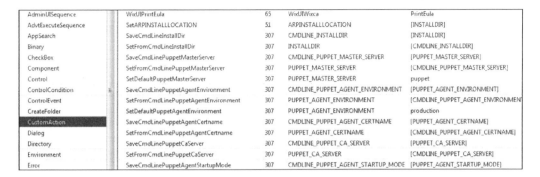

We will change the following three parameters here, and set their values to the Puppet Master FQDN:

- `SaveCmdLinePuppetMasterServer`
- `SetFromCmdLinePuppetMasterServer`
- `SaveCmdLinePuppetAgentEnvironment`

Here are the details after setting the values:

Action	Type	Source	Target
WixUIValidatePath	65	WixUIWixca	ValidatePath
WixUIPrintEula	65	WixUIWixca	PrintEula
SetARPINSTALLLOCATION	51	ARPINSTALLLOCATION	[INSTALLDIR]
SaveCmdLineInstallDir	307	CMDLINE_INSTALLDIR	[INSTALLDIR]
SetFromCmdLineInstallDir	307	INSTALLDIR	[CMDLINE_INSTALLDIR]
SaveCmdLinePuppetMasterServer	307	CMDLINE_PUPPET_MASTER_SERVER	puppetmaster.example.com
SetFromCmdLinePuppetMasterServer	307	PUPPET_MASTER_SERVER	puppetmaster.example.com
SetDefaultPuppetMasterServer	307	PUPPET_MASTER_SERVER	puppetmaster.example.com
SaveCmdLinePuppetAgentEnvironment	307	CMDLINE_PUPPET_AGENT_ENVIRONMENT	[PUPPET_AGENT_ENVIRONMENT]
SetFromCmdLinePuppetAgentEnvironment	307	PUPPET_AGENT_ENVIRONMENT	[CMDLINE_PUPPET_AGENT_ENVIRONMENT]

After the changes are complete, we just save the file and exit. Now we have a file with custom installation parameters. This MSI can be used for bulk installations. We can use this with third-party software or with a domain policy to install it on multiple hosts.

Using software to push the agents

After modifying the MSI file according to our needs, the second step is to install it on the clients and servers that we have. We already have the option to install it on one system at a time. However, this is really not desirable and requires a lot of manual work. So, we need to find a way to push the installation.

We will use the **PDQ Deploy** to distribute the agent. The PDQ Deploy has a trial version and is enough for our needs. To download the application, go to `http://www.adminarsenal.com/pdq-deploy`. This will ask you to fill a short form with your name, surname, e-mail, and, company details. After filling this, you will get the download link. Download the application and install it. It needs .NET 4.0, or above, to run. Even if you don't have .NET, it will be installed. After the PDQ Deploy is installed, run it and it will start with a welcome screen:

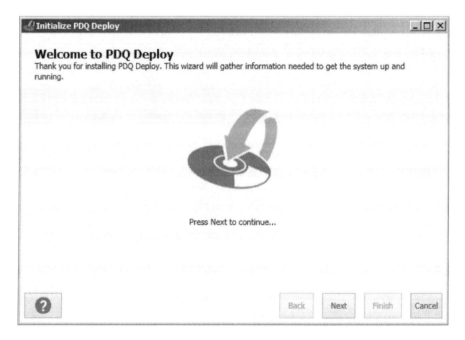

Continue with **Next** and select **Use Free Mode** in the next screen. After this, it will ask for credentials:

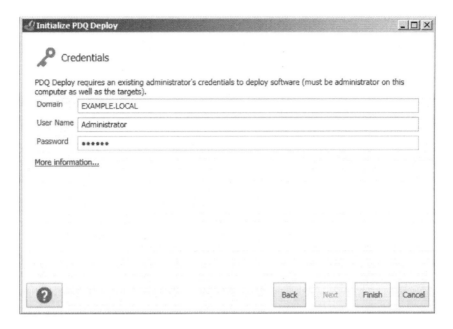

Now, we are on the screen to deploy our agent. Click **Create a new Package** from this screen:

In the package details screen, enter the name as Puppet Agent and the version information for your agent:

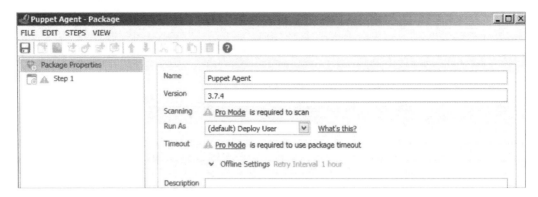

After this, go to **Step 1** on the left-hand side menu:

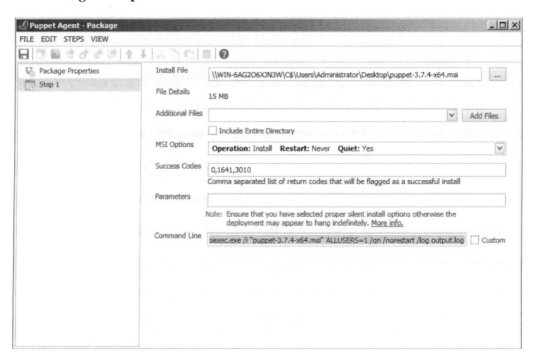

First, select the install file. Ensure that the MSI options are as follows:

- **Operation: Install**
- **Restart: Never**
- **Quiet: Yes**

When the details are complete, click the save icon in the top left of the screen. Now you will have a new **Puppet Agent** package on the screen. Right-click on it and select **Deploy Once**. In the next screen, we need to select our target computers. There are many options for this. You can select them from **Active Directory** in your PDQ library (where there is a list of already used computers), from a target list, or even from a text file. Also, you have the option to add the IPs of the hosts one by one:

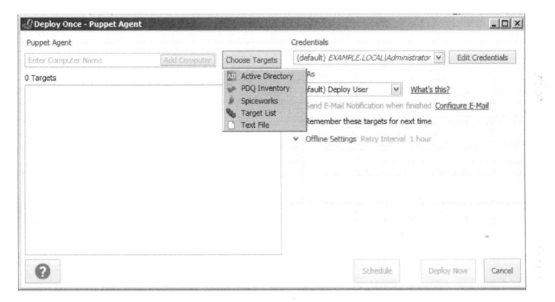

For this example, we will use **Active Directory**, which fits best to the needs of a Windows system administrator. In the testing environment, there are only two Windows 7 hosts connected to the server and these two will be used as examples:

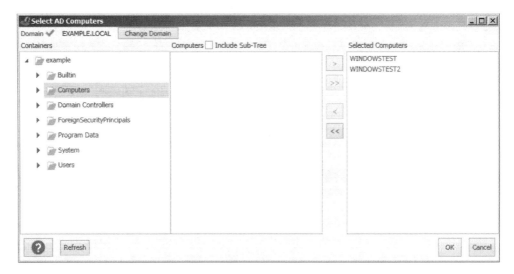

After we are done, we can click **Deploy Now** and see the progress. As you can see, it provides the list of targets and statuses. The deployment of the two hosts took 17 seconds to run, and then finished successfully:

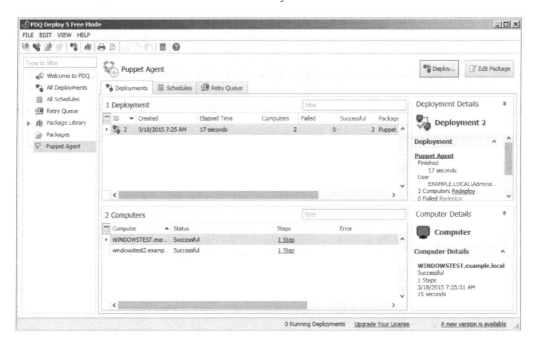

Now, let's check the Windows test host to see whether everything is fine. In the following screenshot, we can see that the installation is successful and there are the details in the **Start** menu. Also, when we check from the Command Prompt, it can be seen that the host is successfully connected and is waiting for certificate signing. The following screenshot shows the successful installation:

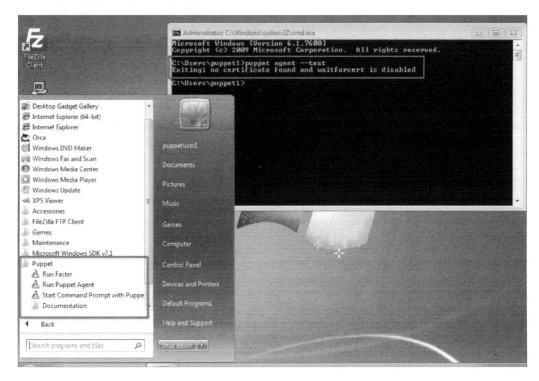

To make sure that the host has connected to the Puppet Master, we can check whether the certificate has been generated. In the certificate details, we can see that the new hosts are waiting to be signed:

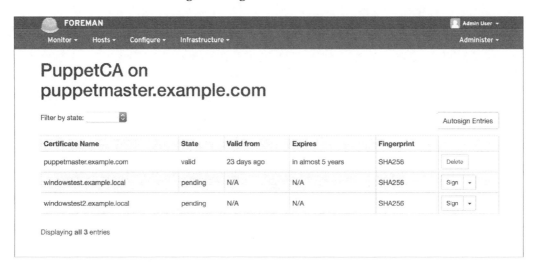

With the PDQ Deploy's free version, we can deploy hundreds or thousands of hosts in one shot. It is also good to see the success and failure details. If there are failures, we can handle them manually or try again by focusing on the problematic ones.

Using a domain controller to push the agents

Windows administrators may prefer to install software through a group policy and may not like the option to use third-party tools. So this is our second option. You can use your own preferred method.

We will use our domain controller's group policy to install the MSI package of the Puppet agent on all the domain servers and client computers. First, place your installation file in a folder and share this folder. The sharing needs to have *Everyone* read rights. We will use the network share link for the group policy, so that the installation file is accessible to everyone.

Here is the share link for this example:

`file://WIN-6AG2O6XJN3W/Users/Administrator/Desktop/puppet.`

From the **Start** menu, **Administrative Tools**, we will run **Group Policy Management**. Here, you can find your domain name. Right-click on the domain name and select **Create a GPO in this domain, and Link it here...**:

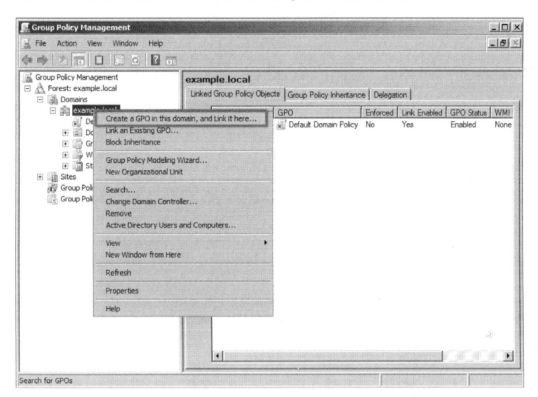

For this example, we will use **PuppetAgent** as the policy name. After creating the policy object, go to the scope details and add **Domain Users**, and also, remove **Authenticated Users**:

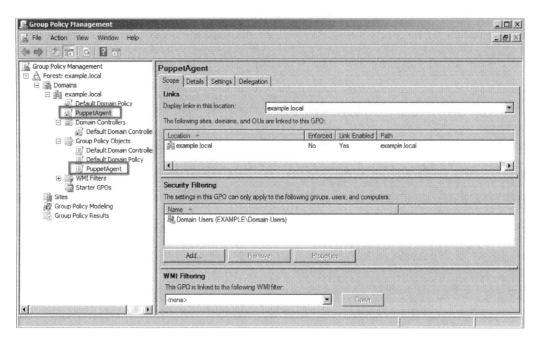

Now, right-click on the **PuppetAgent** object and select **Edit**. Here, go to **User Configuration | Policies | Software Settings | Software installation**. On the right-hand side white space, right-click and select **New | Package**:

You can select **Computer Configuration** here, and the agent can be installed on all your computers without any user dependency. However, the installation will be applied after getting the policy and restarting the relevant computers.

In the new window, we need to select the installation file. We have already created a shared folder, and now we will select it. A shared folder will guarantee that everybody has access to the installation file. In the following screenshot, you can see that the network share is selected:

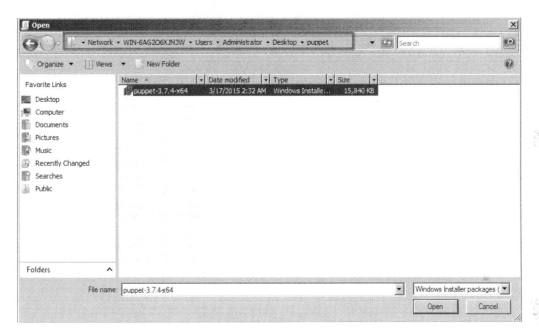

Click **Open** and in the next window, select the **Advanced** radio button and click **OK**. A new window will open. Go to the **Advanced** tab. Select the **Assigned** radio button and the **Install this application at logon** checkbox:

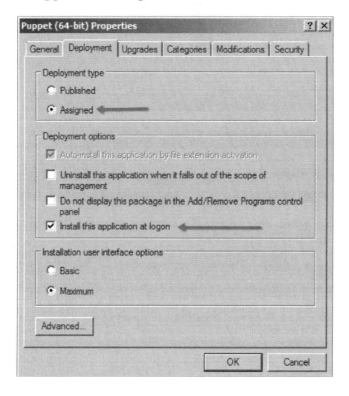

Now we have finished. For the installations to start, first the domain computers have to get the policy. After the policy update, the Puppet agent will be installed at the first logon. The status of the certificates in Foreman will be as shown in the following screenshot. As you can see, we have only one host and that is, Puppet Master (the previous configurations and certificates are removed for testing purposes):

To verify whether the configuration was successful and to make it quicker, we will manually make a policy update. To update the policy, manually run the following command in the Command Prompt of Windows. gpupdate is used for the group policy update. The force parameter forces for an update:

```
C:\>gpupdate /force
```

The policy update shows a warning that there is an update that will be implemented after logoff and logon. We will answer this with Y:

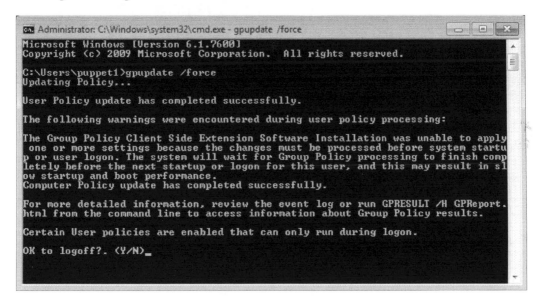

After logon, let's check whether the Puppet agent is installed. As you can see from the **Start** menu, it has been successfully installed:

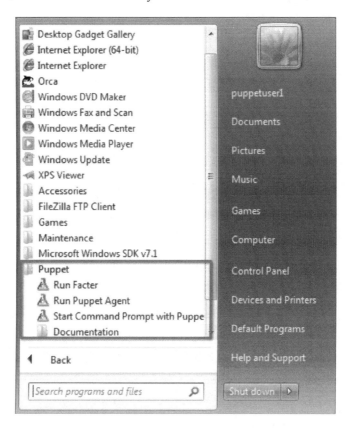

We are done with the `windowstest` host. Now, let's just restart `windowstest2` to verify whether it also gets the policy and installs the agent. After restarting, try logging in to `windowstest2` and check whether the agent shows that the installation was again successful.

Our last step is to check Foreman for the certificates. As you can see in the following screenshot, this step was also successful. Here, we only need to sign the certificates as the last step:

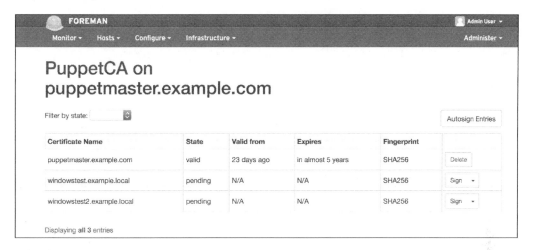

Managing the node certificates

One of the important areas that we need to cover is the management of the host certificates. Puppet uses certificates for a secure connection between the Puppet Master and the hosts. Without signing the certificates, it is not possible to manage any host. For the management of the certificates, we have the following two options:

- Using the Foreman UI
- Using the Puppet Master server terminal with SSH

Displaying the certificates

Let's start with the Foreman UI, which we are already familiar with. In the previous section, *Signing the certificate*, we already added a host and signed its certificate. To refresh our memory, let's do it again.

Go to **Infrastructure | Smart Proxies** from the top menu. In the next screen, click on **Certificates**. As you can see in the following screenshot, we have four hosts at the moment. One of them has been already signed and the others are waiting to be signed:

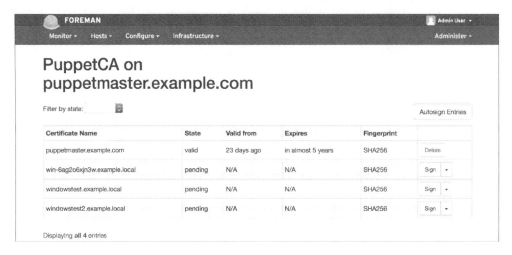

Now, let's check this from the terminal. The commands are as follows:

- `$ sudo puppet cert list --all` **puppet cert**: This command is used for the Puppet certificate management

- `list`: This option lists the certificates that are not signed yet

- `--all`: This option also lists the signed certificates

From the following screenshot, we can see the output. The signed certificates have a plus sign at the beginning of the line:

```
puppet@puppetmaster:~$ sudo puppet cert list --all
  "win-6ag2o6xjn3w.example.local" (SHA256) AD:08:8F:AE:8E:59:EC:CF:5B:90:82:5F:8B:9B:D8:BC:0F:C0:04:6A:20:5A:31:95:C6:8B:88:FF:3B:A9:1E:E7
  "windowstest.example.local"     (SHA256) 4E:EE:FC:C2:C9:9F:98:C2:B5:DD:7B:A3:97:A1:30:AD:41:67:C4:FE:A9:6B:8C:E9:1C:E6:84:C3:13:77:A1:21
  "windowstest2.example.local"    (SHA256) 03:A0:E8:AF:32:73:31:4A:71:6A:FB:09:7B:C2:05:DC:30:72:16:3D:CD:92:37:57:98:DA:9C:03:58:CA:6E:95
+ "puppetmaster.example.com"      (SHA256) 7F:76:66:98:F6:94:56:AD:F8:07:24:7A:CA:9B:80:51:2C:07:62:B4:98:B0:FC:88:74:B0:84:01:0C:0A:67:5D (
alt names: "DNS:puppet", "DNS:puppet.example.com", "DNS:puppetmaster.example.com")
puppet@puppetmaster:~$
```

Signing the certificates

In Foreman, just click the **Sign** button for the relevant host and it will be signed. To do this from the terminal, here is the command:

```
$ sudo puppet cert sign hostname
```

The following is the output to sign a host certificate:

```
puppet@puppetmaster:~$ sudo puppet cert sign windowstest.example.local
[sudo] password for puppet:
Notice: Signed certificate request for windowstest.example.local
Notice: Removing file Puppet::SSL::CertificateRequest windowstest.example.local at '/var/lib/puppet/ssl/ca/requests/windowstest.example.loca
l.pem'
puppet@puppetmaster:~$
```

Deleting the certificates

From Foreman, it is very simple to delete the certificates. If the certificate is already signed, there will be a **Delete** button. If it is not signed yet, you can click the small downward arrow just to the right of the **Sign** button and click **Delete**:

To delete from the terminal, the command is as follows:

```
$ sudo puppet cert clean hostname
```

The following is the output of a certificate deletion:

```
puppet@puppetmaster:~$ sudo puppet cert clean windowstest.example.local
[sudo] password for puppet:
Notice: Revoked certificate with serial 6
Notice: Removing file Puppet::SSL::Certificate windowstest.example.local at '/var/lib/puppet/ssl/ca/signed/windowstest.example.local.pem'
Notice: Removing file Puppet::SSL::Certificate windowstest.example.local at '/var/lib/puppet/ssl/certs/windowstest.example.local.pem'
puppet@puppetmaster:~$
```

If you want to delete the host certificate from the host computer, you can delete the SSL folder under C:\ProgramData\PuppetLabs\puppet\etc\. If you delete both the certificates from the host and the server, the Puppet agent will create a new certificate in the next run. This is useful for problem certificates.

The host groups

The host groups are used for the management of different computer groups. For example, we can create a group for the servers and another group for the clients, or we can create different groups for each department such as finance, human resources, and information technology. If you have different needs for different hosts, then it makes sense to create groups and assign the relevant hosts to them.

For our example, we will keep it simple and create two host groups for the servers and the clients. After this, we will also create subgroups.

Managing the host groups

From the top menu, we select **Configure | Host Groups**. From the new screen, we select the **New Host Group** button. We need to fill the following:

- **Name**: Name of the group.
- **Environment**: We only have the production environment at the moment, and we are selecting it.
- **Puppet CA**: This is the server for the Puppet certificate authority server. In our case, it is same as the Puppet Master.
- **Puppet Master**: This is the Puppet server.

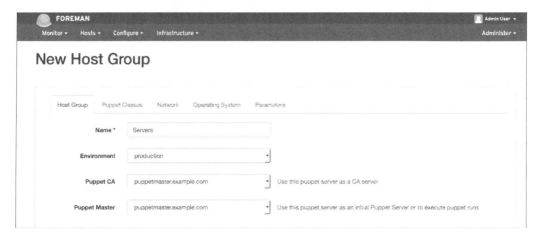

After entering all the details, click the **Submit** button, and your first host group will be saved. Now, we will create another group of clients. This time you will see that there is one new selection, which is `Parent`. This means that you can create subgroups.

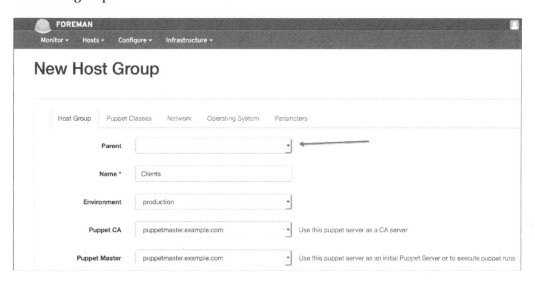

After this, we will create two child host groups: `Windows Servers` and `Linux Servers`. While creating these, we need to select **Servers** as a parent group. When you select a parent, the child will inherit the details from it:

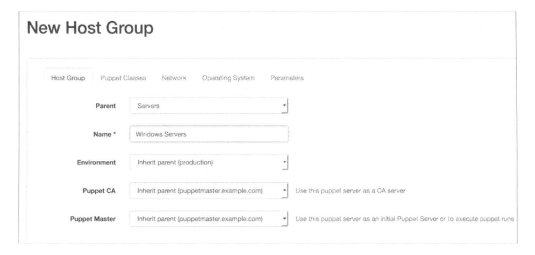

After creating all the groups for our scenario, we can see all these groups in the following screenshot. From the button in each line, we can handle different tasks as follows:

- **Nest**: Create a child group for the relevant group
- **Clone**: Clone the group
- **Delete**: Delete the group

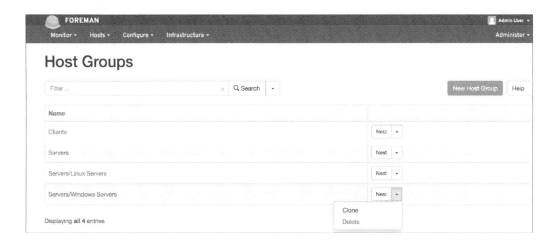

Assigning the hosts to hosts groups

From the top menu, we go to **Hosts | All Hosts**, select the relevant hosts, and use **Select Action | Change Group** to assign the hosts to a group:

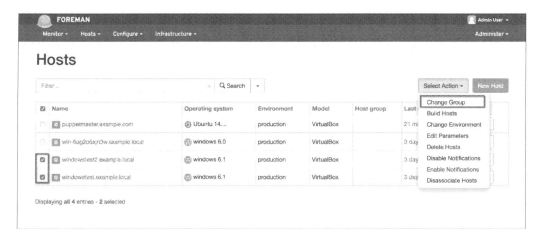

As you can see in the following screenshot, we have selected two of the clients and assigned them to the **Clients** group.

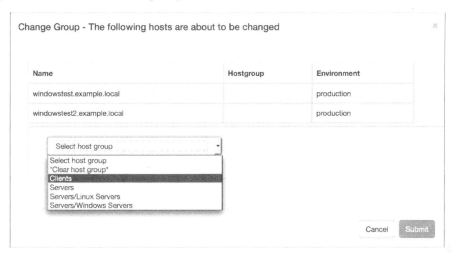

After finishing all the assignments here, we can see all the hosts and their host groups:

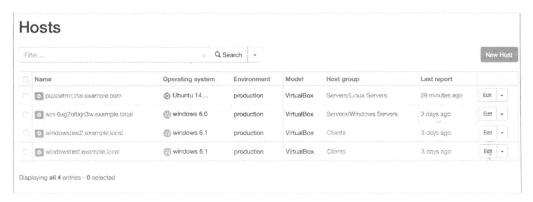

Summary

In this chapter, we first learned how to install Puppet agents on a single computer. Next, we learned how to modify an MSI package, so that we can use it for a silent install. After this, we used the MSI file to install the Puppet agents on multiple hosts using either third-party software or domain group policy.

After finishing the installations, we continued with the management of the host certificates. Finally, we learned how to manage the host groups.

In the next chapter, we will begin to write our first modules to manage the hosts.

3
Your First Modules

In the previous chapter, we learned the installation of Puppet agents on multiple hosts. Now, we will start writing our first modules. We will cover the following topics in this chapter:

- Module structure and defining modules
- Modules to create files and directories
- Assigning classes to hosts and hosts groups
- Modules to manage services
- Modules to manage users
- Modules to run commands

The module structure

We will start with the basic module structure. Puppet uses manifests to apply settings to hosts. Puppet manifests are the files containing the Puppet code. The manifests, files, and data are packed as a module structure. You can write your own modules or you can download pre-built open source modules from the Puppet Forge. We will deal with Puppet Forge modules in *Chapter 4, Puppet Forge Modules for Windows*.

The module layout

A module is simply a directory tree with the following structure:

- `manifests`: This contains the manifests in the module
- `files`: This folder contains the static files that are used by the module

- `templates`: This contains templates that will be used by the Puppet manifests
- `lib`: This contains plugins, such as custom facts and resource types

After the basic structure definition, we will start with our first modules in the next section.

 Because each module needs to have an `init.pp` file with a class name the same as its module, we will see that in Foreman the class names are exactly same as the module names.

You can also create a module with the `puppet generate module` command. The following are the details of how to write the command. For more details, please refer to `https://docs.puppetlabs.com/puppet/latest/reference/modules_fundamentals.html#writing-modules`. The command is as follows:

`puppet module generate <USERNAME>-<MODULE NAME>`

Modules for creating the files and folders

Now, we are starting with our first module definition. The first will be a very easy one. On all the hosts, we will create a file with the content, `Hello World!`, under the `C:\ Windows\Temp>` directory.

The Hello World module

To write our first module, we will connect to the Puppet Master with SSH. The working directory for Puppet modules is `/etc/puppet/modules`. The following is the screenshot of the `/etc/puppet` directory:

```
puppet@puppetmaster:/etc/puppet$ ls -l
total 52
-rw-r--r-- 1 root          root    4179 Feb 23 19:42 auth.conf
-rw-rw-r-- 1 foreman-proxy puppet     0 Feb 23 19:42 autosign.conf
drwxr-xr-x 6 puppet        root    4096 Feb 23 19:42 environments
-rw-r--r-- 1 root          root    1462 Jan 27 01:46 fileserver.conf
-rw-r----- 1 root          puppet   348 Feb 23 19:42 foreman.yaml
drwxr-xr-x 2 root          root    4096 Feb 23 19:42 manifests
drwxr-xr-x 2 root          root    4096 Jan 27 01:48 modules
-r-xr-x--- 1 puppet        puppet  9850 Feb 23 19:42 node.rb
-rw-r--r-- 1 root          root    2605 Feb 23 20:04 puppet.conf
drwxr-xr-x 4 puppet        root    4096 Feb 23 19:42 rack
drwxr-xr-x 2 root          root    4096 Jan 27 01:48 templates
puppet@puppetmaster:/etc/puppet$
```

As we can see from the screenshot, the modules folder is owned by the root. Thus, we will switch to the root account to continue working with the modules directory. The following command will give you the root credentials and will also keep you in the directory you are working:

```
$ sudo -s
```

If you are not yet at the correct directory, just use the cd command to go to /etc/puppet/modules:

```
# cd /etc/puppet/modules
```

Creating the directory structure

The next step is to create our module structure. The most basic one has the following:

- One directory with the module name
- Another directory, under the module name, named manifests

We will use the mkdir command to create the directories. Here is a sample screenshot:

```
root@puppetmaster:/etc/puppet/modules# mkdir helloworld
root@puppetmaster:/etc/puppet/modules# cd helloworld/
root@puppetmaster:/etc/puppet/modules/helloworld# mkdir manifests
root@puppetmaster:/etc/puppet/modules/helloworld# cd ..
root@puppetmaster:/etc/puppet/modules# tree helloworld/
helloworld/
└── manifests

1 directory, 0 files
root@puppetmaster:/etc/puppet/modules#
```

 If the tree command does not work, it can be installed using apt-get install tree.

Creating the manifest file

After completing the directory structure, the next step is to create the manifest file. For a module, we need to create the init.pp file under the manifests file. init. pp file contains the class definition for the module. The class name and the module name should be the same. To create the new file, you can use the Nano text editor:

```
# cdhelloworld/manifests
```

```
# nanoinit.pp
```

The class name must be the same as the module name. The following is the class definition:

```
classhelloworld {


}
```

Now, we will define the file that will be created. In the following code snippet, you can see the very basic definition of this:

```
file { 'path and name of file':
content => "Content of file",
}
```

The following are the details of the `manifests`:

```
1 class helloworld {
2   file { 'c:/windows/temp/hello.txt':
3     content => "Hello World!",
4   }
5 }
```

- **Line 1**: This defines the class name
- **Line 2**: This defines the file path and name
- **Line 3**: This defines the content of the file
- **Lines 4** and **5**: These end the class and file definitions

We have finished the creation of our first module. Now, we will continue in Foreman and import the module class. After the import, we can use the class for our hosts or host groups.

 In line **2** of code snippet in the preceding screenshot, for path definition, we used the forward slash / symbol. Normally, in Windows, the backslash \ symbol is used. However, backslash is an escape sign in Linux. Puppet correctly works with forward slashes on Windows. Thus, while defining the file paths, we can use /.

Importing the module class in Foreman

Log in to the Foreman user interface. From the top menu go to **Configure | Puppet classes**. After this, click on the **Import from yourserveraddress** button. For our example in this book, the button is **Import from puppetmaster.example.com**.

After clicking on the button, we will see our newly created module name. You will also see the different environments: **common**, **development**, **example_env**, and **production**. As you will recall, we assigned all our hosts to the production environment. We will do the same and assign the module to the production environment. To do this, just click on the checkbox in the **production** line and after this click on the **Update** button:

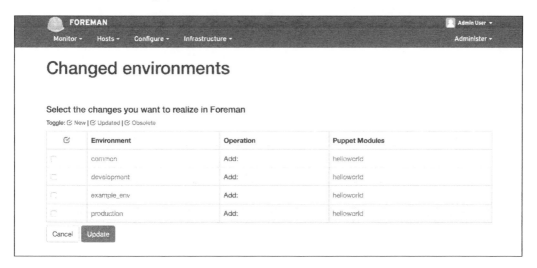

We are using only the production environment to keep things simple. In the real world, it will be a good idea to use the development and production environments. The development environment can be used to test your modules. When you feel comfortable, you can assign the module to the production environment and the relevant hosts.

To keep this even simpler, you can use /etc/puppet/ environments/production/, so that the class appears only in the production environment while you are trying to import it. However, in live environments, it will be easier to first put it under /etc/puppet/modules. First, import into the development test and after this, import into production.

After the successful import of the module, you will see your module class under the
Puppet classes:

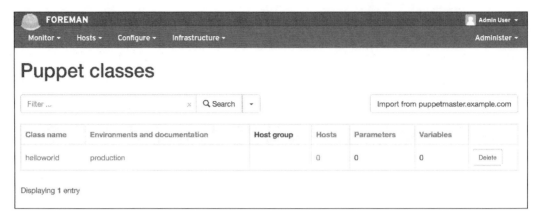

Assigning the class to a host

We have imported the class and now we will assign it to a host. To do this, we will
browse to all the lists of the hosts and select one of them by clicking the **Edit** button.
For this example, we will continue with **windowstest.example.local**:

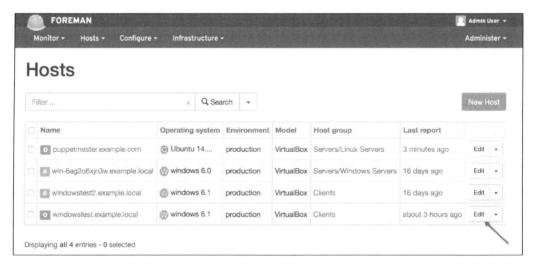

In the host details complete the following steps:

1. Click the **Puppet Classes** tab.

2. Click the little grey-colored plus button near the module name.

3. Click on the black-colored plus button. This will assign the **helloworld** module to the host. To save your changes, click on the **Submit** button in the bottom-left corner of the page:

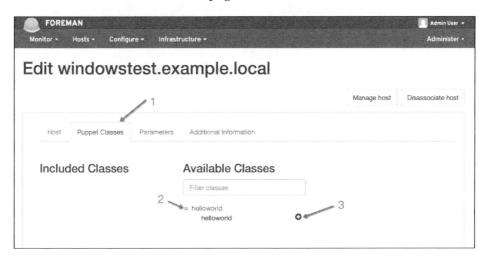

We are done with assigning our module to a host. The last step is to test and see whether everything works fine. To check, follow these steps:

1. Go to your host and open a Command Prompt with administrator rights. Run the `puppet agent --test` command.

2. Open a Windows Explorer window and check the `C:\Windows\Temp\` folder for the `hello.txt` file.

In the following screenshot, we can see that our first module and the file creation is successful:

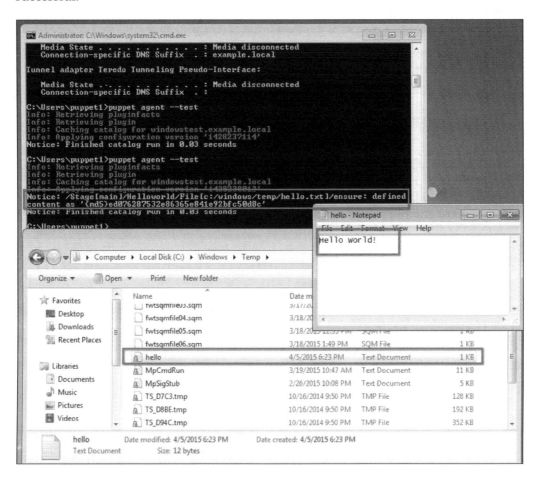

Assigning the class to a host group

Assigning the class to a host group is almost the same as assigning it to a host. First, go to **Configure | Host Groups** from the top menu. Click one of the listed host groups. For this example, we can use the **Clients** group. Click the **Clients** group and follow the same steps that you followed while assigning a module to a host.

To check if the class is assigned to the hosts in a host group, we will check the details of **windowstest2**. In the host lists, click on **Edit** for **windowstest2** and go to the **Puppet Classes** tab. As you can see in the following screenshot, the **helloworld** class is assigned to the host. However, there is no "minus" button near the class and it cannot be removed at the host level. This is because it is assigned at the host group level:

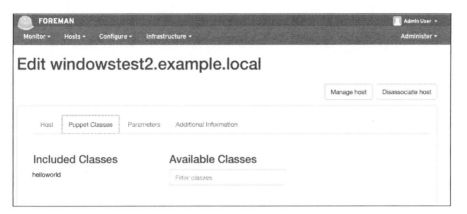

Uploading files

If you have a very long text file or a binary file, it really does not make sense to use the content option. In this case, we will directly refer to the file and it will be uploaded. Later, if we make any changes in our file in the server, this change will be also applied to all the hosts.

Here is the definition:

```
file { 'path and name of file':
source => 'puppet:///modules/modulename/filename',
}
```

We will, again, use the `hello.txt` file, but this time we will create the details under our module. For this purpose, create the `files` folder under the `helloworld` module. After this, create the `hello.txt` file under the `files` folder.

The module structure is as shown in the following screenshot, and we can also see the contents of the hello.txt file:

```
root@puppetmaster:/etc/puppet/modules# tree helloworld/
helloworld/
├── files
│   └── hello.txt
└── manifests
    └── init.pp

2 directories, 2 files
root@puppetmaster:/etc/puppet/modules# cat helloworld/files/hello.txt
Hello World!
File example
root@puppetmaster:/etc/puppet/modules#
```

The next step now is to change our init.pp file. The following are the details of the init.pp file. Just be aware that we are not using the files folder in the source definition:

```
GNU nano 2.2.6                    File: helloworld/manifests/init.pp

class helloworld {
  file { 'c:/windows/temp/hello.txt':
    source => 'puppet:///modules/helloworld/hello.txt',
  }
}
```

As we have already imported the module class in Foreman, we do not need to repeat the steps. Now, we can just have a test run and see the results, as follows:

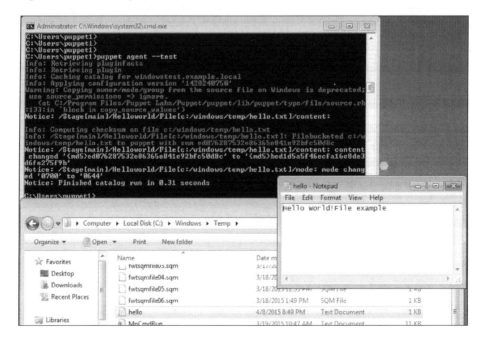

As you can see, these results are fine. Puppet checks the md5 hash of the file to see whether it is different. You can see in the preceding screenshot that it says **content changed** from one md5 to another. However, we only have a tiny problem.

Copying the file permissions from the source is deprecated for Windows. We can just remove this warning by adding additional details in the file definition. We need to add a line, source_permissions => ignore. Here are the new details:

```
 GNU nano 2.2.6              File: helloworld/manifests/init.pp

class helloworld {
  file { 'c:/windows/temp/hello.txt':
    source => 'puppet:///modules/helloworld/hello.txt',
    source_permissions => ignore,
  }
}
```

Now just make a change in hello.txt and run the test again. There will be no warning, as shown here:

```
C:\Users\puppet1>puppet agent --test
Info: Retrieving pluginfacts
Info: Retrieving plugin
Info: Caching catalog for windowstest.example.local
Info: Applying configuration version '1428241504'
Notice: /Stage[main]/Helloworld/File[c:/windows/temp/hello.txt]/content:

Info: Computing checksum on file c:/windows/temp/hello.txt
Info: /Stage[main]/Helloworld/File[c:/windows/temp/hello.txt]: Filebucketed c:/w
indows/temp/hello.txt to puppet with sum bed1d5a5f46ecfa16e8de3d6fe275f9b
Notice: /Stage[main]/Helloworld/File[c:/windows/temp/hello.txt]/content: content
 changed '{md5}bed1d5a5f46ecfa16e8de3d6fe275f9b' to '{md5}1ed755edfa285cc951e2d5
f74d6a7447'
Notice: Finished catalog run in 0.34 seconds

C:\Users\puppet1>
```

Creating folders

For creating folders, we again use the file definition. The details are as follows:

```
file { 'folder':
ensure => 'directory',
source_permissions => ignore,
  }
```

Now, let's create a `helloworld` folder in the `helloworld` class. Here are the details:

```
GNU nano 2.2.6                    File: helloworld/manifests/init.pp

class helloworld {
  file { 'c:/windows/temp/hello.txt':
    source => 'puppet:///modules/helloworld/hello.txt',
    source_permissions => ignore,
  }
  file { 'c:/windows/temp/helloworld':
    ensure => 'directory',
    source_permissions => ignore,
  }
}
```

Here are the test run details. As you can see, the `helloworld` folder was created successfully:

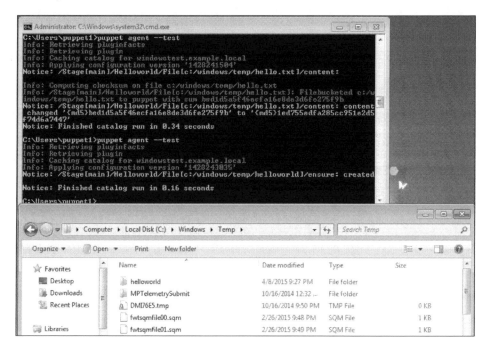

Managing services

Puppet resource type `service` is used to manage services. In Windows, the management capabilities are somewhat limited. However, if we want to make sure that a service always runs or always stops, we can use the `service` type.

Here is how to write this:

```
service { 'servicename':
ensure =>running,stopped
enable =>true,false,manual
    }
```

The following points explain the preceding code:

- First line is the service name in Windows.

- `ensure => running` makes sure that the service is running. You can also use `stopped` option to make sure that the service is not running.

- `enable => true` ensures that the service will autostart after a reboot. The `false` option ensures that the service is disabled. Lastly, the `manual` option sets the starting of the service to manual.

As an example, let's start with disabling the Windows file and print sharing features. You can see the service details in the following screenshot. The service display name is **Server** and the service name is **LanmanServer**. We will disable this service on all client machines, so that the users cannot use print and file sharing:

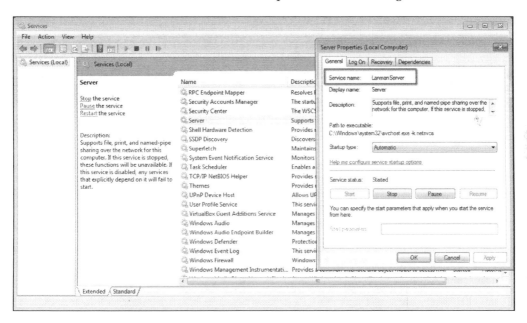

We will also create a module for this. The following is the module structure:

```
root@puppetmaster:/etc/puppet/modules# mkdir disablesmb
root@puppetmaster:/etc/puppet/modules# mkdir disablesmb/manifests
root@puppetmaster:/etc/puppet/modules# touch disablesmb/manifests/init.pp
root@puppetmaster:/etc/puppet/modules# tree disablesmb/
disablesmb/
└── manifests
    └── init.pp

1 directory, 1 file
root@puppetmaster:/etc/puppet/modules#
```

The only command that we did not mention in the preceding screenshot is the `touch` command. This command creates empty files with the specified name. The manifest details are as follows:

```
  GNU nano 2.2.6                         File: disablesmb/manifests/init.pp

class disablesmb  {
  service { 'LanmanServer':
    ensure  => stopped,
    enable  => false,
  }
}
```

As you can see in the preceding screenshot, we defined a new class and module named `disablesmb`. We made sure that it is stopped and disabled. After this, we will import the new class to Foreman and assign it to the **Clients** host group. If you need help with these steps, please check out the previous section, *Modules for creating the files and folders*. Now, let's move on to testing of the Puppet agent to see the results:

```
C:\Users\puppet1>puppet agent --test
Info: Retrieving pluginfacts
Info: Retrieving plugin
Info: Caching catalog for windowstest.example.local
Info: Applying configuration version '1420245198'
Error: Cannot stop LanmanServer, error was: Execution of 'C:/Windows/system32/ne
t.exe stop LanmanServer' returned 4294967295: The following services are depende
nt on the Server service.
Stopping the Server service will also stop these services.

   Computer Browser

Do you want to continue this operation? (Y/N) [N]:
No valid response was provided.
Wrapped exception:
Execution of 'C:/Windows/system32/net.exe stop LanmanServer' returned 4294967295
: The following services are dependent on the Server service.
Stopping the Server service will also stop these services.

   Computer Browser

Do you want to continue this operation? (Y/N) [N]:
No valid response was provided.
Error: /Stage[main]/Disablesmb/Service[LanmanServer]/ensure: change from running
 to stopped failed: Cannot stop LanmanServer, error was: Execution of 'C:/Window
s/system32/net.exe stop LanmanServer' returned 4294967295: The following service
s are dependent on the Server service.
Stopping the Server service will also stop these services.

   Computer Browser

Do you want to continue this operation? (Y/N) [N]:
No valid response was provided.
Notice: Finished catalog run in 1.19 seconds

C:\Users\puppet1>_
```

As we can see in the preceding screenshot, there is a dependent service, **Computer Browser**. We need to stop this, if we want to continue. So, we will define another service detail. Also, we need to make sure that, first **Computer Browser** stops, and after this the `Server` service stops. When we check the service name, it is `Browser`, so here are the details:

```
GNU nano 2.2.6                    File: disablesmb/manifests/init.pp

class disablesmb  {

  service { 'Browser':
    ensure  => stopped,
    enable  => false,
  }

  service { 'LanmanServer':
    ensure  => stopped,
    enable  => false,
    require => Service['Browser'],
  }
}
```

As you can see in the preceding screenshot, we first defined the `'Browser'` service and then stopped it. However, Puppet does not run `manifests` in an ordered top to down fashion. So we added to our `'LanmanServer'` service definition a new line, `require`. This definition will only run after the `'Browser'` service definition. The uppercases and lowercases are also important. You should be careful while writing a `require` line.

The `require` definition from Puppet Labs: `require` causes a resource to be applied after the target resource.

Now let's test this again:

```
C:\Users\puppet1>puppet agent --test
Info: Retrieving pluginfacts
Info: Retrieving plugin
Info: Caching catalog for windowstest.example.local
Info: Applying configuration version '1428246001'
Notice: /Stage[main]/Disablesmb/Service[Browser]/ensure: ensure changed 'running'
' to 'stopped'
Notice: /Stage[main]/Disablesmb/Service[LanmanServer]/ensure: ensure changed 'ru
nning' to 'stopped'
Notice: Finished catalog run in 9.28 seconds

C:\Users\puppet1>
```

As we can see, this time it ran without any errors. Now let's check the service details and whether it has been stopped and disabled:

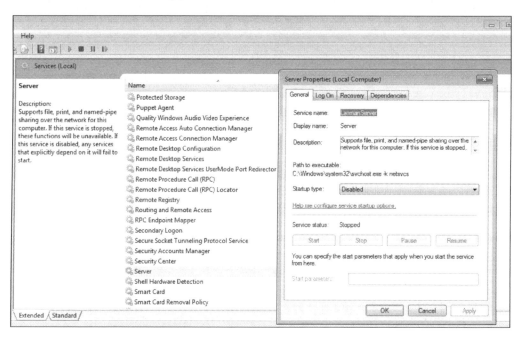

As you can see in the preceding screenshot, the service has been stopped and disabled. You can use the same logic to enable and make sure a service is running. For example, it is a good practice to enable and again run the stopped antivirus services.

Running commands

The `exec` resource type is used to execute commands. The command in the `exec` resource must be able to run multiple times without any problems or harm. If it causes problems, it must be limited with conditions and run only when these conditions are met.

`exec` can directly execute `.com`, `.bat`, `.exe`, and so on. Also, it can log the output and the exit status. If you want to run the shell built-in commands in this case, Puppet does not support these commands directly. Assuming that you want to use the `echo` command, you need to use it with `cmd` and the command should look as follows: `cmd.exe /c echo helloworld`. Now let's check the most basic definition:

```
exec { 'execname':
command => 'command to execute',
}
```

As you can see, the simplest `exec` definition requires only one attribute, which is `command`. This command will execute every time Puppet runs. The default running interval for Puppet is 30 minutes. So, if the default interval is not changed, it will be executed every 30 minutes.

The following is the definition in detail. These are not the full details. If you need more details, please refer to `https://docs.puppetlabs.com/`:

```
exec { 'resource title':
command     => # (namevar) The actual command to execute.
creates     => # A file to look for before running the command.
path        => # The directory of command.
logoutput   => # Whether to log command output
refreshonly => # The command should only be run as a refresh.
returns     => # The expected exit code(s).  Any different exit code
will return error.
timeout     => # The maximum time the command should take.
}
```

Now let's write our module class. As an example we will write a simple clean-up manifest that deletes the unnecessary files. To keep it simple, we will delete only the files and folders under `C:\Windows\Temp`. Here are the details:

The module structure is as follows:

```
root@puppetmaster:/etc/puppet/modules# tree cleanuppc/
cleanuppc/
└── manifests
      └── init.pp

1 directory, 1 file
```

The manifest details are as follows:

```
cleanup windows
class cleanuppc {
  exec { 'deltemp':
    command => 'cmd.exe /C del /Q /F /S C:\Windows\Temp\*.*',
    path    => 'C:\Windows\System32',
  }
}
```

In the preceding screenshot, the command lines are as follows:

- **Line 1**: The comment about the class.
- **Line 2**: The class definition and its name.
- **Line 3**: The `exec` type definition.
- **Line 4**: The command to be executed:
  - In this line `cmd.exe /C` is to execute the shell built-in command, `del`
  - The `del` command has many parameters here: `/Q` for going into quite mode and asks for no confirmation, `/F` forces to delete anything even it is read-only, and `/S` deletes subdirectories
- **Line 5**: This is the path for `cmd.exe`.

Now let's test this. Here are the `C:\Windows\Temp` details before the Puppet run:

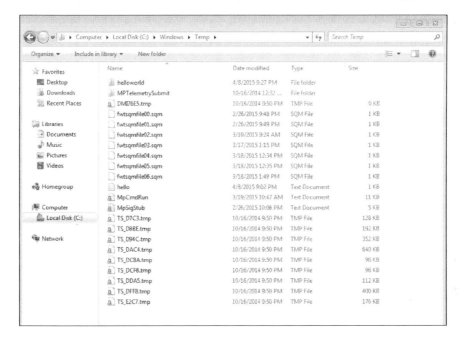

Here are the test run results and folder details:

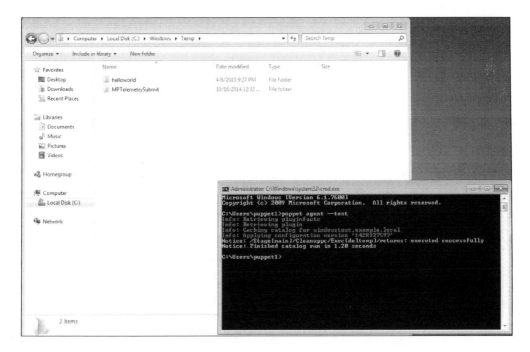

Running the command on certain conditions

If you want to run the command only once or whenever a condition is met, you can use the `creates` and `refreshonly, subscribe` attributes.

The `creates` attribute will create a file and when this attribute sees the file in the next run, the command will not execute. So, the command will run only when the specified file does not exist. Here is a sample code:

```
# cleanup windows
classcleanuppc {
exec { 'deltemp':
command => 'cmd.exe /C del /Q /F /S C:\Windows\Temp\*.*',
path    => 'C:\Windows\System32',
creates=> 'C:\testfile.txt',
   }
}
```

One important point is here that, the file will not be created by Puppet. So, if only the command or some other software, which you have checked, creates this file, the `creates` attribute will be useful. Otherwise, the command will continue to run each time.

For the `refreshonly` attribute, the command will bind to another resource with `subscribe`. Here is the example code:

```
# cleanup windows
class cleanuppc {
  exec { 'deltemp':
    command    => 'cmd.exe /C del /Q /F /S C:\Windows\Temp\*.*',
    path       => 'C:\Windows\System32',
    subscribe  => File['c:/windows/temp/helloworld'],
    refreshonly => true,
  }
}
```

The `subscribe` attribute binds this `exec` command to the `helloworld` folder creation in our `helloworld` module that we created previously. `refreshonly` makes sure that it will only run manually. The following is the test run:

```
C:\Users\puppet1>puppet agent --test
Info: Retrieving pluginfacts
Info: Retrieving plugin
Info: Caching catalog for windowstest.example.local
Info: Applying configuration version '1428929108'
Notice: /Stage[main]/Helloworld/File[c:/windows/temp/helloworld]/ensure: created

Info: /Stage[main]/Helloworld/File[c:/windows/temp/helloworld]: Scheduling refre
sh of Exec[deltemp]
Notice: /Stage[main]/Cleanuppc/Exec[deltemp]: Triggered 'refresh' from 1 events
Notice: Finished catalog run in 1.20 seconds

C:\Users\puppet1>
```

As you can see, this time the command is triggered by an event.

As a final detail, there is also a native Puppet resource, tidy, to clean up the unnecessary files. Even if we write our own code to clean up a folder, it will be a good practice to stick to native resource types whenever possible. tidy removes the unnecessary files according to a given criteria. Here is a class definition example:

```
classcleanuppc {tidy { 'deltemp ':
path=> "C:/Windows/Temp/",
recurse=> 1,
matches => [ "*.*" ]
  }

}
```

For more information, you can check the following link: https://docs.puppetlabs.com/references/latest/type.html#tidy.

Managing users

The user resource type is used to manage the local users. It was first built for Linux systems, so it has its limitations. The following is the list of attributes that can be used for Windows. One of the important limitations is that, Puppet can manage the local users (not domain users). The attributes are as follows:

- name: The user name.
- ensure: The state of the user (present, or absent).
- comment: The description of the user, usually the full name.
- groups: The groups that the user will be assigned. Note that you can't use the gid attribute.
- home: The home directory of the user. This folder needs to be created separately.
- manage home: If this value is set to true, it will create the home directory when the user is created, and will delete the home directory, if the user is set to absent.
- password: Note that passwords can only be specified in clear text, since Windows has no API to set the password hash.

After covering the details, here is an example definition:

```
user { 'testuser':
ensure => 'present',
name => 'puppetuser',
comment => 'Puppet User',
groups => [ 'Administrators', 'Users' ],
password => 'Qwer1234',
}
```

In the preceding example, we define a user resource named 'testuser'. This resource creates a Windows user named 'puppetuser'. This user is a member of the 'Administrators' and 'Users' groups. The user has a comment, 'Puppet User'.

One more important point is that, in attributes you can use more than one value using arrays. For array definitions, you can use [and]. We used an array for the preceding groups.

Also, we need to add this resource definition to a module so that it is usable. For our example, we will create a module named createuser. The following is the module structure:

```
root@puppetmaster:/etc/puppet/modules# tree createuser/
createuser/
└── manifests
    └── init.pp

1 directory, 1 file
```

The following screenshot shows the sample class. You may notice that the code is colored. If you use vim as the editor, it will display the manifest code in color. Also, we added a comment line in the manifest. You can use the # symbol to add the comment lines:

```
# creates puppetuser
class createuser {
  user { 'testuser':
    ensure   => 'present',
    name     => 'puppetuser',
    comment  => 'Puppet User',
    groups   => [ 'Administrators', 'Users' ],
    password => 'Qwer1234',
  }
}
```

Now, after completing the import and assignments in Foreman, we can test the module. The following are the test run details:

```
C:\Users\puppet1>puppet agent --test
Info: Retrieving pluginfacts
Info: Retrieving plugin
Info: Caching catalog for windowstest.example.local
Info: Applying configuration version '1428248130'
Notice: /Stage[main]/Createuser/User[testuser]/ensure: created
Notice: Finished catalog run in 0.20 seconds

C:\Users\puppet1>
```

We can see that the test run returns a successful result. Now let's check whether the user really exists. In the following screenshot, we can see that the user is created as a local user:

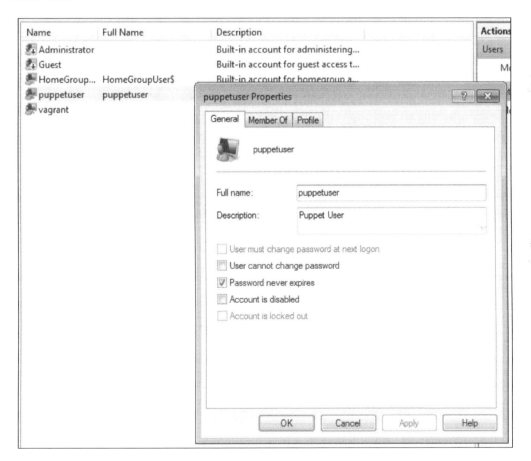

In the following screenshot, we can see that the groups are also correctly set:

We are done with the user creation. Also, you can try yourself the `ensure =>` `'absent'` option to remove a user.

Summary

In this chapter, first we learned how to install and create our modules, and import the classes into Foreman. After the import, we assigned the classes to hosts and hosts groups.

We also learned the different types of resources and their usages, such as creating files and folders, managing services, running commands, and managing users.

In the next chapter, we will learn about the Puppet Forge modules for Windows.

4
Puppet Forge Modules for Windows

Puppet Forge is a website that is used to share the Puppet modules. The website is
`https://forge.puppetlabs.com`. There is good documentation of Puppet Forge
that explains how to write your own modules on Puppet docs. You can find the
details at `http://docs.puppetlabs.com/forge/`. There are lot of modules written
to solve the daily administration and configuration problems. Before starting to write
a specific module for yourself, it is a good place to check whether your needs are
already covered by a module in Puppet Forge.

There are different levels of certification for modules in Puppet Forge. The best level
is the **Supported level**. Supported means that:

- The module is tested by Puppet Enterprise
- It is subject to the Puppet Enterprise support
- It will be maintained over the life cycle of the module with bug and
  security patches
- It will be tested and ensured that it is compatible with multiple platforms

Another level is **Approved**. Approved means that the modules meet the Puppet Labs'
standards of quality composition, reliable operation, and active development. What is
missing for the Approved modules is, that Puppet does not give enterprise support.

In this chapter, we will learn about the following:

- Installing modules from Puppet Forge
- Managing the registry with the registry module
- Managing file and folder permissions with the **Access Control List
  (ACL)** module

- Managing the firewall rules with an unsupported module example
- Rebooting Windows with the reboot module

Installing modules from Puppet Forge

Installing the Puppet modules from Puppet Forge is very easy and can be done using only one command, as follows:

```
$ sudo puppet module install modulename
```

If you are using the Puppet environment, you can also use the following command:

```
$ puppet module install -i /etc/puppet/environments/production/modules
modulename
```

The only thing we need to know here, is the module name. For example, let's search for the **registry** module to see what we get. The details are given as follows:

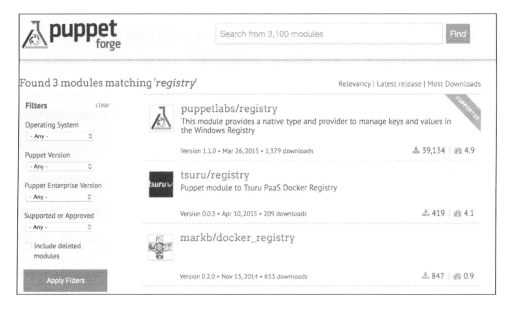

As you can see, we have the **puppetlabs/registry** supported module. After clicking on this, we can use the following command to install it:

The supported and approved modules also have the documentation and examples in the module page. You can see the documentation table of contents in the following screenshot:

Managing the registry

In the previous topic, we learned how to install a module from Puppet Forge. The example was on the `registry` module. The command to install the `registry` module is as follows:

```
$ sudo puppet module install puppetlabs-registry
```

```
puppet@puppetmaster:/etc/puppet/modules$ ls -l
total 16
drwxr-xr-x 3 root root 4096 Apr 13 10:22 cleanuppc
drwxr-xr-x 3 root root 4096 Apr  5 18:10 createuser
drwxr-xr-x 3 root root 4096 Apr  5 17:35 disablesmb
drwxr-xr-x 4 root root 4096 Apr  5 16:17 helloworld
puppet@puppetmaster:/etc/puppet/modules$ sudo puppet module install puppetlabs-registry
[sudo] password for puppet:
Notice: Preparing to install into /etc/puppet/modules ...
Notice: Downloading from https://forgeapi.puppetlabs.com ...
Notice: Installing -- do not interrupt ...
/etc/puppet/modules
└── puppetlabs-registry (v1.1.0)
    └── puppetlabs-stdlib (v4.6.0)
puppet@puppetmaster:/etc/puppet/modules$ ls -l
total 24
drwxr-xr-x 3 root root 4096 Apr 13 10:22 cleanuppc
drwxr-xr-x 3 root root 4096 Apr  5 18:10 createuser
drwxr-xr-x 3 root root 4096 Apr  5 17:35 disablesmb
drwxr-xr-x 4 root root 4096 Apr  5 16:17 helloworld
drwxr-xr-x 7 root root 4096 Mar 26 19:44 registry
drwxr-xr-x 6 root root 4096 Apr 15  2015 stdlib
puppet@puppetmaster:/etc/puppet/modules$
```

As you can see in the preceding screenshot, the new module is installed. The `stdlib` module was also installed. As we can see, it is a dependency for `registry`. `stdlib` is used to add the library resources for Puppet. We will deal with `stdlib` later in functions and facts.

> After the installation, we again need to import these modules to Foreman. When we check the new modules, we will see that only `stdlib` is available. This is not an error. The `registry` module does not have an `init.pp` file under manifests folder, so the module cannot be directly imported. However, we still can use it.

As an example, we will create a new module that makes sure that the Windows Firewall is active and all three profiles are running. Here is the current status of the firewall in our sample client:

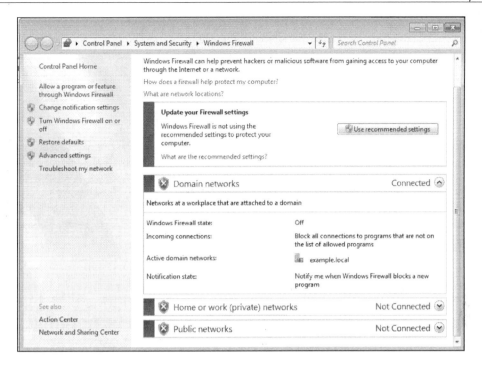

As you can see, all the **Domain networks, Home or work (private) networks,** and **Public networks** profiles are disabled.

The details to change in the registry are under `HKLM\SYSTEM\CurrentControlSet\Services\SharedAccess\Parameters\FirewallPolicy\`. There are three folders and settings that have to be changed. You can see the details in the following screenshot:

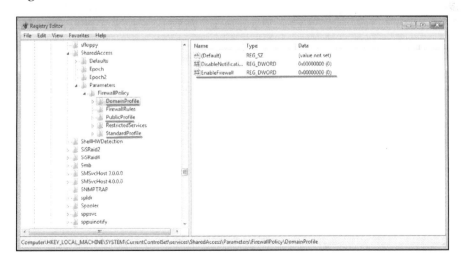

We need to change each of the **EnableFirewall** value to 1 for **DomainProfile**, **PublicProfile**, and **StandardProfile**. After precisely setting the firewall keys, the changes will be effective after the Windows reboot.

Writing the manifests

Here is an example code, and the matched fields are shown in the following screenshot:

```
registry::value { 'firewalldomain':
key   => 'HKLM\SYSTEM\CurrentControlSet\Services\SharedAccess\
Parameters\FirewallPolicy\DomainProfile',
value => 'EnableFirewall',
type  => 'dword',
data  => '1',
}
```

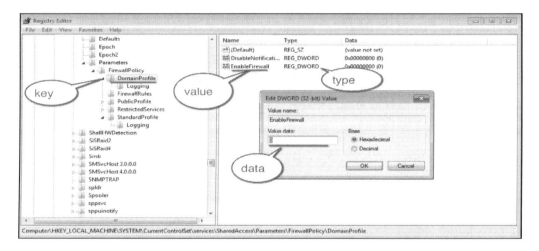

As you can see, the entire folder is the **key** field. The details in the folder are **value** and the assigned detail in **value** is **data**. Also, we need to be careful about the type, otherwise we may corrupt the firewall settings.

Now, we can start writing our module. The module name is `firewallon`. Here are the manifest details:

```
# enable windows firewall profiles
class firewallon {
  registry::value { 'firewalldomain':
    key   => 'HKLM\SYSTEM\CurrentControlSet\Services\SharedAccess\Parameters\FirewallPolicy\DomainProfile',
    value => 'EnableFirewall',
    type  => 'dword',
    data  => '1',
  }

  registry::value { 'firewallstandard':
    key   => 'HKLM\SYSTEM\CurrentControlSet\Services\SharedAccess\Parameters\FirewallPolicy\StandardProfile',
    value => 'EnableFirewall',
    type  => 'dword',
    data  => '1',
  }

  registry::value { 'firewallpublic':
    key   => 'HKLM\SYSTEM\CurrentControlSet\Services\SharedAccess\Parameters\FirewallPolicy\PublicProfile',
    value => 'EnableFirewall',
    type  => 'dword',
    data  => '1',
  }
}
```

Here are the test run details:

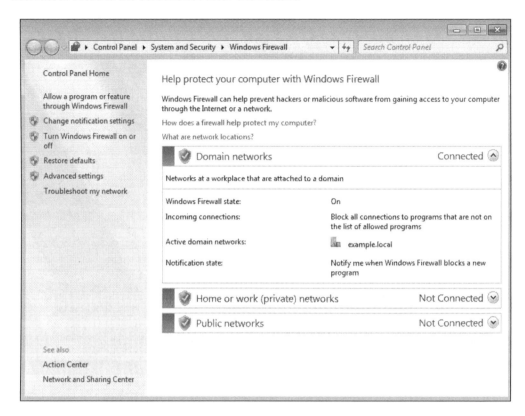

 We can also start the firewall service with the service type. You can try this yourself. After setting the correct values, you can enable the **Windows Firewall** service and this will enable the firewall without a restart.

Limitations with the registry module

Before finishing this section, we need to mention that there are some limitations with the registry module. The supported keys are as follows:

- `HKEY_LOCAL_MACHINE` (hklm)
- `HKEY_CLASSES_ROOT` (hkcr)

Other predefined root keys (for example, `HKEY_USERS`) are not currently supported. Finally, Puppet does not support recursive deletion of the registry keys.

The access control list

The ACL module manages the **Access Control Lists** in Windows. The Linux way of giving rights to folders and files does not work correctly in Windows. The ACL module adds a type provider to Puppet. We can use this `acl` type to assign permissions and rights to files and folders.

To install `acl`, you need to write the following command:

```
$ sudo puppet module install puppetlabs-acl
```

Here are the definition details of an `acl`:

```
acl { 'name':
target=> 'absolute/path',
target_type=> '<file>',
purge=> '<true| false | listed_permissions>',
permissions=> [
{ identity=> '<identity>',
rights=> [<rights>],
perm_type=> '<perm_type>',
affects=> '<affects>',
child_types => '<child_types>'
}
],
owner=> '<owner>',
group=> '<group>',
inherit_parent_permissions => '<true | false>',
}
```

Here are the details of the each parameter and attribute:

- `name`: The name of the ACL resource. If the target is not defined, this can be also used as a target.

- `target`: The location of the ACL resource.

- `target_type`: The only valid value is `file`. No need to define this one.

- `purge`: The valid values are `true`, `false`, and `listed_permissions`. The default is `false`. We can use this parameter to make sure that some of the permissions are absent. To do this, we need to use the `listed_permissions` option. This parameter will not affect the permissions inherited from the parents.

- `inherit_parent_permissions`: To remove the `parent` permission, `inherit_parent_permissions => 'false'` can be used. However, you can lock the folder completely. So, you may need to modify each host manually to re-enable the folder.

- `group` and `owner`: We can set the `owner` and `group` of the file or folder with this attribute.

- `permissions`: This is an array of the **Access Control Entries (ACE)**. The ACEs must be in explicit and correct order.

- `identity`: This can be a user, group or SID.

- `rights`: This is also an array. The valid values are `full`, `modify`, `mask_specific`, `write`, `read`, and `execute`.

- `mask`: The `mask` is an element that only works, if `'mask_specific'` is set in the `rights` element. The value must be an integer representing the `mask` permissions passed in to a string. For more details about "integer representing mask permissions", please visit `https://msdn.microsoft.com/en-us/library/aa394063(v=vs.85).aspx`.

- `perm_type`: This can be `'allow'` or `'deny'`, and it defaults to `'allow'`.

- `child_types`: This determines how an ACE is inherited downstream from the target. The valid values are `'all'`, `'objects'`, `'containers'` or `'none'`. It defaults to `'all'`.

- `affects`: This determines how the downstream inheritance is propagated. The valid values are `'all'`, `'self_only'`, `'children_only'`, `'self_and_direct_children_only'`, or `'direct_children_only'`. This defaults to `'all'`.

After covering all the details, we can continue with the examples. First, as you can see, there are default values and we do not need to use most of the preceding parameters. Let's start with a simple example.

Changing the permissions of a folder

In this example, we have a `C:\testacl` folder. The details can be seen as follows. Under this folder, there is an empty file named `test.txt`. `test.txt` inherits the permissions from its parent and the details are same as its parent folder:

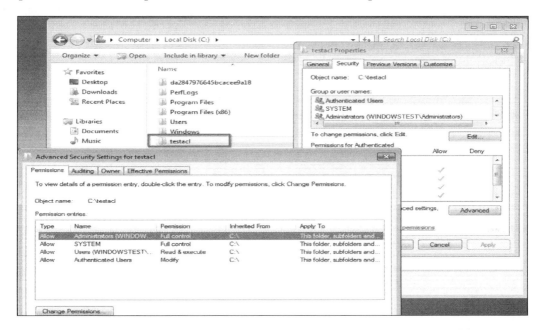

In our example, we will create a new user named `testy` and assign full rights to it. As you will recall, we already learned how to create users. If you need to remember the details, you can go to *Chapter 3, Your First Modules* to refresh your memory.

Here is a sample code to give the permissions. As you can see, it is very simple. Only the folder name, user, and permission details are defined. All the other values that are not defined will be the default values:

```
acl { 'c:/testacl':
permissions => [
{ identity => 'testy', rights => ['full'] },
],
}
```

As an example module, we will use `acltestmodule` as a module name. Here is a sample structure of it:

```
root@puppetmaster:/etc/puppet/modules# tree acltestmodule/
acltestmodule/
└── manifests
    └── init.pp

1 directory, 1 file
root@puppetmaster:/etc/puppet/modules#
```

Here are the manifest details:

```
# creates testy user and makes ACL assignments
class acltestmodule {
  user { 'testy':
    ensure      => 'present',
    name        => 'testy',
    comment     => 'testy user for ACL',
    groups      => [ 'Users' ],
    password    => 'Qwer1234',
  }
  acl { 'c:/testacl':
    permissions => [
      { identity => 'testy', rights   => ['full'] },
    ],
    require      => User['testy'],
  }
}
```

In the previous manifest, we have also put a require line. This will prevent any errors about the user and make sure that, firstly the user creation runs and after this, the relevant permissions are set.

After running the test, its details will be as follows:

```
C:\Users\puppet1>puppet agent --test
Info: Retrieving pluginfacts
Info: Retrieving plugin
Info: Loading facts
Info: Caching catalog for windowstest.example.local
Info: Applying configuration version '1429871901'
Notice: /Stage[main]/Acltestmodule/User[testy]/ensure: created
Notice: /Stage[main]/Acltestmodule/Acl[c:/testacl]/permissions: permissions chan
ged [
] to [
  { identity => 'WINDOWSTEST\testy', rights => ["full"] }
]
Notice: Finished catalog run in 0.27 seconds

C:\Users\puppet1>
```

As we can see, first the user is created and after this, the permissions are set. Our next step is to check the folder and file to see whether the rights are correctly set.

The `C:\testacl` permissions are as follows:

As we can see in the following screenshot, the permissions are applied to all the sub-objects:

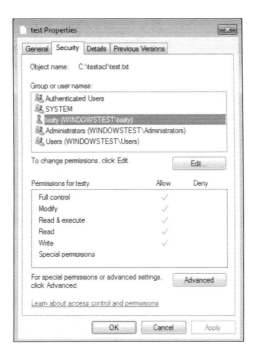

Purging permissions

After many trials, it is understood that for the current Puppet 3.7.4 version, the `purge => 'listed_permissions'` option is not working properly. So we need to do this the hard way:

- First, set the `purge => true` option.

- Second, set `inherit_parent_permissions => 'false'`, so that nothing is inherited.

- Third, define all the default permissions that are required:

```
permissions => [
{ identity => 'SYSTEM', rights => ['full'], child_types => 'all'
},
{ identity => 'Administrators', rights => ['full'] },
{ identity => 'Authenticated Users', rights => ['read','execute']
},
],
```

- Finally, define the extra permissions you want to add, excluding the ones you want to remove.

Here is the sample code:

```
# creates testy user and makes ACL assignments
class acltestmodule {
  user { 'testy':
    ensure    => 'present',
    name      => 'testy',
    comment   => 'testy user for ACL',
    groups    => [ 'Users' ],
    password  => 'Qwer1234',
  }

  acl { 'C:\testacl':
    purge => true,
    permissions => [
      { identity => 'SYSTEM', rights => ['full'], child_types => 'all' },
      { identity => 'Administrators', rights => ['full'] },
      { identity => 'Authenticated Users', rights => ['read','execute'] },
      { identity => 'testy', rights   => ['execute','read'] },
    ],
    inherit_parent_permissions => false,
    require    => User['testy'],
  }
```

In this example, we used the same module limiting the `testy` user's rights to `read` and `execute`. As we are purging all the permissions and not inheriting any, we set all the required permissions manually.

Keep in mind that using `purge => true` and `inherit_parent_permissions => 'false'` together and not setting the permissions correctly, may cause the relevant files and folders to be locked. You may need to manually connect and correct the permissions.

Purging permissions and locking a file from user changes

If you want to lock a file or folder from any user changes, you can lock with the following code:

```
acl { 'C:\testacl':
purge => true,
permissions => [
{ identity => 'SYSTEM', rights => ['full'], child_types => 'all' },
{ identity => 'Administrators', rights => ['full'] },
],
inherit_parent_permissions => false,
}
```

In this example, only the SYSTEM user and Administrators can change the folder. All other user permissions are removed.

Firewall

First of all, there is no supported or approved module for the Windows Firewall management. We will use `puppet/windows_firewall` as an example. The link to the module details is `https://forge.puppetlabs.com/puppet/windows_firewall`. When we use the unsupported modules, the problem is that it may not work as expected. However, we can check the code details and create our own modules accordingly.

Here are some details of this module:

- When you try to enable the firewall, it does not enable all the profiles. While testing Windows 7, it did not enable the domain profile.

- When the rule with the same name already exists, it will do nothing. So when you want to change an existing rule, this will not work.

- When `ensure => absent` is used, it gives error and does not work correctly.

- So this module is good only to add new rules.

This example module is given here to learn that when we use unsupported ones, they need to be tested carefully. Otherwise, we may have many problems. We may still use these modules to check the code details and create our own modules.

To install the module, we can use the following command:

```
$ sudo puppet module install puppet-windows_firewall
```

The firewall rule example

We will create an example that creates a rule that only allows certain IPs to connect to the 3389 port.

Here is the sample code:

```
classfirewallrules {
windows_firewall::exception { 'WINRM':
ensure         => present,
direction      => 'in',
action         => 'allow',
enabled        => 'yes',
protocol       => 'TCP',
local_port     => '3389',
remote_ip      => '10.10.10.20,10.10.10.21',
display_name   => 'Windows RDP Rule allowips',
description    => 'Inbound rule for Windows RDP allow [TCP 3389]',
}
}
```

Here are the details of the preceding code:

- direction: The values are 'in' for the incoming traffic and 'out' for the outgoing traffic.
- action: The values are 'allow' and 'block'.
- enabled: The value can be 'yes' or 'no'.
- protocol: TCP, UDP, ICMP and so on are available.
- local_port: The port or ports. These are the ports to which we are allowing access.

- `remote_ip`: The remote IP or IPs that will be defined.
- `display_name`: The name of the rule.
- `description`: The description of the rule.

Here is the module structure:

```
root@puppetmaster:/etc/puppet/modules# tree firewallrules
firewallrules
└── manifests
    └── init.pp

1 directory, 1 file
root@puppetmaster:/etc/puppet/modules#
```

Here is the manifest example:

```
# ensure firewall is running and add rules
class firewallrules {
  windows_firewall::exception { 'WINRM':
    ensure       => present,
    direction    => 'in',
    action       => 'allow',
    enabled      => 'yes',
    protocol     => 'TCP',
    local_port   => '3389',
    remote_ip    => '10.10.10.20,10.10.10.21',
    display_name => 'Windows RDP Rule allow ips',
    description  => 'Inbound rule for Windows RDP allow [TCP 3389]',
  }
}
```

Here are the run details:

```
C:\Users\puppet1>puppet agent --test
Info: Retrieving pluginfacts
Info: Retrieving plugin
Info: Loading facts
Info: Caching catalog for windowstest.example.local
Info: Applying configuration version '1429896122'
Notice: /Stage[main]/Firewallrules/Windows_firewall::Exception[WINRM]/Exec[set r
ule Windows RDP Rule allow ips]/returns: executed successfully
Notice: Finished catalog run in 2.36 seconds

C:\Users\puppet1>
```

Here is the new rule in the firewall details:

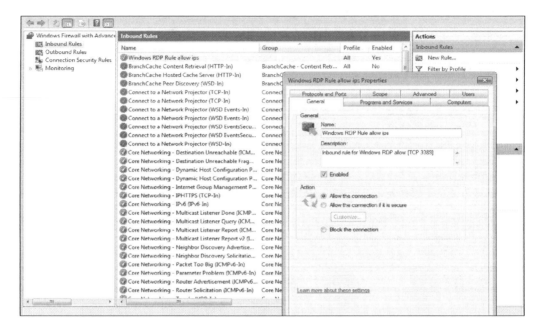

The reboot module

This module adds a type to reboot Windows and Linux systems. It is supported by Puppet Enterprise. We possibly need time to reboot our systems. We cannot use reboot without any conditions. Otherwise, each run will cause a reboot and everybody will start complaining about the reboots. So, it is a good practice to limit these with a `notice` or `register` option.

The URL for the `puppetlabs/reboot` module is `https://forge.puppetlabs.com/puppetlabs/reboot`. To install this, simply run the following command on a terminal:

```
$ sudo puppet module install puppetlabs-reboot
```

Following is a sample `reboot` definition. In this example, the `reboot` subscribes to a file creation. Whenever `testfile.txt` is created, it will trigger the `reboot`:

```
reboot { 'name':
subscribe => File['c:/testfile.txt'],
}
```

Now, let's see this in an example. We will create a simple module that creates a file. Whenever this file is created, it will trigger a reboot. Our example module name is testreboot. The structure is as follows:

```
root@puppetmaster:/etc/puppet/modules# tree testreboot/
testreboot/
└── manifests
    └── init.pp

1 directory, 1 file
root@puppetmaster:/etc/puppet/modules#
```

Here are the manifest details:

```
# test example for reboot
class testreboot {
  file { 'c:/windows/temp/testreboot.txt':
    content          => 'Testing reboot',
    source_permissions => ignore,
  }
  reboot { 'restartexample':
    subscribe        => File['c:/windows/temp/testreboot.txt'],
  }
}
```

We can see the following result screen of the test run:

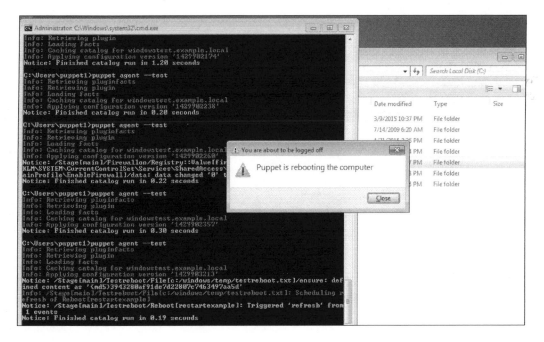

After the restart, running Puppet again does not trigger a reboot. It will only reboot again, whenever `c:/windows/temp/testreboot.txt` is missing.

```
Administrator: C:\Windows\system32\cmd.exe
Microsoft Windows [Version 6.1.7600]
Copyright (c) 2009 Microsoft Corporation.   All rights reserved.

C:\Users\puppet1>puppet agent --test
Info: Retrieving pluginfacts
Info: Retrieving plugin
Info: Loading facts
Info: Caching catalog for windowstest.example.local
Info: Applying configuration version '1429903359'
Notice: Finished catalog run in 0.22 seconds

C:\Users\puppet1>
```

The `testreboot` and `cleanuppc` class together may cause a reboot each time the Puppet agent runs. This happens because `cleanuppc` deletes the contents of the `C:Windows\Temp folder`, and `testreboot` runs, if it does not see the `testreboot.txt` file under `C:Windows\Temp`. So, it will be good to remove the assignment of the `cleanuppc` class before testing the `testreboot` class.

Summary

In this chapter, we started with learning what Puppet Forge is and the supported and approved modules. We learned how to install modules from Puppet Forge. The modules that we learned about are: registry, ACL, firewall, and reboot.

In the next chapter, we will dive in to more advanced subjects such as:

- Puppet facts
- Puppet functions
- Puppet templates

5
Puppet Facts, Functions, and Templates

In this chapter, we will learn more advanced details of Puppet such as:

- Puppet facts
- Puppet templates
- Puppet functions

If you are familiar with programming languages, this chapter will be much easier to follow. Puppet uses Ruby as the coding language. We will not dive deep into the coding aspect and will use only enough coding to solve our problems. So, even if you do not have any coding experience, it will not be too hard to follow.

Puppet facts

Facts are structured data about the system that we can use anywhere in our manifests. They are imported to the Puppet parser as top scope variables. To display the facts of a host, we can use the `facter` command. We can write the command as follows to display the host-specific facts in each host's Command Prompt:

```
C:\>facter -p
```

In the following screenshot, we can see a sample output of the command. As we can see, there are many details such as architecture, domain, OS version, interfaces, and IP addresses:

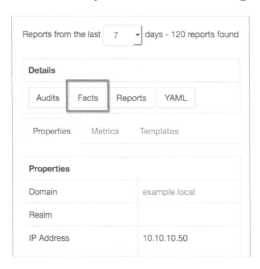

Another easier way to look at the facts is by using our Foreman interface. In the top menu, go to **Hosts | All Hosts** and select the relevant host that you want to check out. Now, click the **Facts** button and you can see the following details:

As you can see in the following screenshot, we have the facts of a host again:

Using the facts in manifests

After learning how to display the facts, now let's continue with how to use them. In our example, we will change our `firewallon` module and it will run only if the host is Windows; when the host is Linux, it will display a predefined message. Here is our example code:

```
if $::osfamily == 'windows' {
...
} else {

}
```

In the preceding code, it will include the code details for Windows when the operating system family is Windows and will include another code when it is not. To display a message we will use `notify`. Following is the sample format:

```
notify {'message':}
```

Here is the example that we will use:

```
notify {"This module runs only for Windows OS family. This host
has OS family $::osfamily installed.":}
```

As you can see, we can also use variables in the text fields. When we use a variable, we also need to use the quotation mark (") instead of an apostrophe (').

The following shows the modified `firewallon` module details:

```
# enable windows firewall profiles
class firewallon {

  if $::osfamily == 'windows' {
    registry::value { 'firewalldomain':
      key   => 'HKLM\SYSTEM\CurrentControlSet\Services\SharedAccess\Parameters\FirewallPolicy\DomainProfile',
      value => 'EnableFirewall',
      type  => 'dword',
      data  => '1',
    }

    registry::value { 'firewallstandard':
      key   => 'HKLM\SYSTEM\CurrentControlSet\Services\SharedAccess\Parameters\FirewallPolicy\StandardProfile',
      value => 'EnableFirewall',
      type  => 'dword',
      data  => '1',
    }

    registry::value { 'firewallpublic':
      key   => 'HKLM\SYSTEM\CurrentControlSet\Services\SharedAccess\Parameters\FirewallPolicy\PublicProfile',
      value => 'EnableFirewall',
      type  => 'dword',
      data  => '1',
    }
  } else {
    notify {"This module runs only for Windows OS family. This host has OS family $::osfamily":}
  }
}
```

Here is the output of a test run when it is assigned to the Puppet Master:

```
root@puppetmaster:/etc/puppet/modules# puppet agent --test
Info: Retrieving pluginfacts
Info: Retrieving plugin
Info: Loading facts
Info: Caching catalog for puppetmaster.example.com
Info: Applying configuration version '1429910747'
Notice: This module runs only for Windows OS family. This host has OS family Debian
Notice: /Stage[main]/Firewallon/Notify[This module runs only for Windows OS family. This host has OS family Debian]/message: defined 'message' as 'This module runs only for Windows OS family. This host has OS family Debian'
Notice: Finished catalog run in 0.19 seconds
root@puppetmaster:/etc/puppet/modules#
```

As you can see, it is not running the module and displaying any messages.

Adding the custom facts

We may also need custom facts. For example, when dealing with users, it is important to know the Windows users and make changes accordingly. We will start with a simple example that shows how to add a custom fact.

This example custom fact is a simple one. We will create a fact named `firstfact` and make its value `Hello World!`. We can add custom facts by modules. In a module structure, it adds the facts under the `lib/facter` folder. To remember where we put our custom facts, we will create a module named `common` and put all our facts in this folder. The name of the module is not important here and you can give it any name. For now, we will just use `common`. Here is the module structure:

```
root@puppetmaster:/etc/puppet/modules# tree common/
common/
├── lib
│   └── facter
│       └── first.rb
└── manifests
```

We will put our custom fact definitions under the `facter` folder and the files must have the `.rb` extension. The name of the file is not important. All the `.rb` files will be processed.

Now, let's continue with the code details of defining a fact:

```
Facter.add("factname") do
setcode do
"factvalue"
end
end
```

As you can see from the preceding code, it is really self-explanatory. We will use `Facter.add` for each fact definition. The following is the example code for `firstfact`:

```
# firstfact definition example
Facter.add("firstfact") do
  setcode do
    "Hello World!"
  end
end
```

We do not need to define our `common` module. The facts will be defined automatically for each host. The following screenshot shows the output of a test run after the fact definition:

```
C:\Users\puppet1>puppet agent --test
Info: Retrieving pluginfacts
Info: Retrieving plugin
Notice: /File[C:/ProgramData/PuppetLabs/puppet/var/lib/facter/first.rb]/content:

Notice: /File[C:/ProgramData/PuppetLabs/puppet/var/lib/facter/first.rb]/content:
 content changed '{md5}0756564d602509f23f6fbb8e3068a85d' to '{md5}3acc0ef00e9109
1907e1e9f7d8274b10'
Info: Loading facts
Info: Caching catalog for windowstest.example.local
Info: Applying configuration version '1429914478'
Notice: Finished catalog run in 0.28 seconds

C:\Users\puppet1>
```

Now, it is time to check whether we have the fact details. The following screenshot shows that the fact is correctly defined and available:

```
Administrator: C:\Windows\system32\cmd.exe

C:\Users\puppet1>facter -p
architecture => x64
dir => C:\Program Files\Puppet Labs\Puppet\facter
domain => example.local
env_windows_installdir => C:\Program Files\Puppet Labs\Puppet
facterversion => 2.3.0
firstfact => Hello World!
fqdn => WINDOWSTEST.example.local
hardwaremodel => x64
hostname => WINDOWSTEST
id => example\puppet1
interfaces => Local_Area_Connection
ipaddress => 10.10.10.50
ipaddress_local_area_connection => 10.10.10.50
is_pe => false
is_virtual => true
kernel => windows
kernelmajversion => 6.1
kernelrelease => 6.1.7600
kernelversion => 6.1.7600
macaddress => 08:00:27:EA:42:24
macaddress_local_area_connection => 08:00:27:EA:42:24
```

Adding Windows users as custom facts

We have learned all about the Puppet facts, how to list them, see the values, and define the custom facts. Now, we come to a more useful fact definition. We will find Windows users and their SID values and put them in the custom facts. We will later need them when we need to do user-specific changes. This is a more advanced topic. However, we will learn many other details when we are done with this.

Here are the steps to find the users:

1. Find the user profile details in the registry.
2. Loop each entry and get the user name and SID details.
3. Put the details in the users and sids arrays and define them as facts.

Again, we will create a file under the common module of the lib/facter folder. We will name it as users.rb. Here is the module structure:

```
root@puppetmaster:/etc/puppet/modules# tree common
common
├── lib
│   └── facter
│       ├── first.rb
│       └── users.rb
└── manifests

3 directories, 2 files
root@puppetmaster:/etc/puppet/modules#
```

Making sure our code works only for Windows

First of all, as this is a Windows-only module, we will add a condition so that it works only for Windows. The code details are given as follows:

```
ifFacter.value(:osfamily) == 'windows'
...
...
end
```

As you can see, this is somewhat different from manifest coding. Here, we are using Ruby. When we refer to a fact, we need to use Facter.value(:factname).

> You do not need to know the Ruby language. I found most of the details from Google search and created my own facts with a little bit coding.

Including the necessary libraries

We will read the Windows Registry, so we need to include the library for this. The command is given as follows:

```
require 'win32/registry'
```

Defining your variables with empty values

We will use two variables, users and sids, and we define them in the beginning with empty values. This is done as follows:

```
users = ''
sids = ''
```

So far, the complete code that we have written is as follows:

```
if Facter.value(:osfamily) == 'windows'
require 'win32/registry'

users = ''
sids = ''

end
```

Finding the registry values

Before reading the registry, we need to know what we have to read and how to parse the data. We will need the values under HKEY_LOCAL_MACHINE\Software\ Microsoft\Windows NT\CurrentVersion\ProfileList. Each key starting with S-1-5-21 is a user SID. Under these keys, each **ProfileImagePath** value has the folder of this user. The following is a screenshot to see this more clearly:

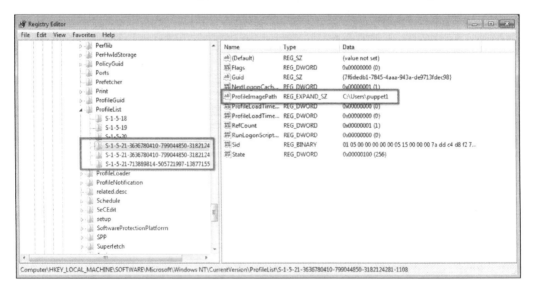

So, we will get the SID value from the keys under **ProfileList** and we will get the username from **ProfileImagePath**. After removing C:\Users\, the rest is the username. After understanding the logic, let's continue with the coding.

This section becomes a little bit complicated, so first we will start with the code and later define each line. Here is the code:

```
 1 if Facter.value(:osfamily) == 'windows'
 2 require 'win32/registry'
 3
 4 users = ''
 5 sids = ''
 6
 7 Win32::Registry::HKEY_LOCAL_MACHINE.open(
 8   'Software\Microsoft\Windows NT\CurrentVersion\ProfileList'
 9 ) do |reg|
10   reg.each_key do |key|
11     k = reg.open(key)
12         profile = k["ProfileImagePath"]
13         len = profile.length
14         len = len - 9
15         user = profile[9,len]
16         if profile[0,8] == 'C:\Users'
17           users = user + ',' + users
18           sids = key + ',' + sids
19         end
20   end
21 end
22
23 end
```

The explanation for the preceding code is as follows:

- Lines **7**, **8**, **9**, and **21** are as follows:

```
Win32::Registry::HKEY_LOCAL_MACHINE.open(
'Software\Microsoft\Windows NT\CurrentVersion\ProfileList'
) do |reg|

end
```

In lines **7**, **8**, `Win32::Registry::HKEY_LOCAL_MACHINE.open` reads the registry details.

In lines **9**, **21**: `do |reg|`

`do-end` is a loop block. Here for each detail from the registry, it will loop and assign the details to the `reg` variable.

Now, we have all the keys and their subdetails in the `reg` variable.

- Lines **10** and **20** are as follows:

```
reg.each_key do |key|

end
```

Here we are looping for each of the registry keys and assigning them to the `key` variable.

- Line **11** is as follows:

```
k = reg.open(key)
```

In this command, as you know, we already have the `reg` variable defined. Also, we defined the `key` variable. Now, we are opening the `key` from `reg` and assigning the details to the `k` variable.

- Line **12** is given as follows:

```
profile = k["ProfileImagePath"]
```

Under the key, there is the **ProfileImagePath** value; read its data and assign it to the `profile` variable. You can see the **ProfileImagePath** value and its data details for one of the users as follows:

- Lines **13**, **14**, and **15** are as follows:

```
len = profile.length
len = len - 9
user = profile[9,len]
```

Here we know that `C:\Users\` is a character string with length 9. We first get the complete length of the `profile` variable in line **13**. After this, we get the length of the username at line **14** and assign it to the `len` variable. Finally from the profile, we get the username at line **15** and assign it to the user variable.

- Lines **16**, **17**, **18**, and **19** are as follows:

```
if profile[0,8] == 'C:\Users'
users = user + ',' + users
sids = key + ',' + sids
end
```

At line **16**, we first check whether the `profile` variable starts with `'C:\ Users'`. If it does not, then we will not use it. At line **17**, we fill the `users` variable with the user details in a comma delimited format. In line **18**, we fill the SIDs. As you will remember, the SID was the key value. So we can directly use it.

Now we have finished the hardest part. We can continue with defining the facts. This is the easiest part as we have already filled our variables with the correct values. Here are the code details for our `users` and `sids` facts:

```
Facter.add("users") do
setcode do
users
end
end

Facter.add("sids") do
setcode do
sids
end
end
```

Here is the complete coding screenshot:

```
if Facter.value(:osfamily) == 'windows'
require 'win32/registry'

users = ''
sids = ''

Win32::Registry::HKEY_LOCAL_MACHINE.open(
  'Software\Microsoft\Windows NT\CurrentVersion\ProfileList'
) do |reg|
  reg.each_key do |key|
    k = reg.open(key)
        profile = k["ProfileImagePath"]
        len = profile.length
        len = len - 9
        user = profile[9,len]
        if profile[0,8] == 'C:\Users'
          users = user + ',' + users
          sids = key + ',' + sids
        end
  end
end

Facter.add("users") do
  setcode do
    users
  end
end

Facter.add("sids") do
  setcode do
    sids
  end
end

end
```

Now we will again run the Puppet agent and check the facts to see whether we get the details. The following is the output of `facter` in one of the Windows hosts and we can see the `users` and `sids` facts:

Now, if you want to get only the relevant fact details, you can also use the following commands:

```
C:\>facter -p users
C:\>facter -p sids
```

As a final notice, this code will work only for the users that are logged in and who have profile details created.

The Puppet templates

Templates are used to specify the contents of files. When we have a file to be created and its content needs to be created dynamically, we use templates. Templates are written in the ERB templating language. ERB is supported by Ruby. You can refer to http://ruby-doc.org/stdlib-1.8.7/libdoc/erb/rdoc/ERB.html for more information. To use a template, we need to create a folder named `templates` under the relevant module. In the `templates` folder, we can use any file name with the `.erb` extension.

We will start with a simple file creation example. As you will remember, our first module was the `helloworld` module and we created a file in the hosts from static content. Now let's go back to this and add some dynamic content.

To refresh our memory, here are the details of the `helloworld` module. The manifest details are as follows:

```
# helloworld class
class helloworld {
  file { 'c:/windows/temp/hello.txt':
    source            => 'puppet:///modules/helloworld/hello.txt',
    source_permissions => 'ignore',
  }
  file { 'c:/windows/temp/helloworld':
    ensure            => 'directory',
    source_permissions => 'ignore',
  }
}
```

As we can see, it is now creating a file and a directory. The file is created from the static content. Here is the module structure:

```
root@puppetmaster:/etc/puppet/modules# tree helloworld/
helloworld/
├── files
│   └── hello.txt
├── manifests
│   └── init.pp
└── templates
    └── hello.erb

3 directories, 3 files
root@puppetmaster:/etc/puppet/modules#
```

We will create a new `templates` directory and under this another `hello.erb` file. After this, it will look as follows:

```
root@puppetmaster:/etc/puppet/modules# tree helloworld/
helloworld/
├── files
│   └── hello.txt
├── manifests
│   └── init.pp
└── templates
    └── hello.erb

3 directories, 3 files
root@puppetmaster:/etc/puppet/modules#
```

Now let's write our simple template. When we write any code in a template, we start with `<%` and end with `%>`. We can also use the facts in templates and any variable that we have defined. To use facts, we add a `@` symbol in front of them. When we want to include the variable value, we use `=` after `<%`. After learning these details, here are the contents of `hello.erb`:

```
Hello World!
I am a computer running <%= @operatingsystem %> as operating
system.
```

As you can see in the preceding code, we have used the `operatingsystem` fact as our dynamic content. Now let's change the manifest accordingly. To define the content of a file from the template, we need to add an attribute to the file resource as follows:

```
content => template('classname/templatefile.erb'),
```

Here is our new manifest accordingly:

```
# helloworld class
class helloworld {
  file { 'c:/windows/temp/hello.txt':
    content            => template('helloworld/hello.erb'),
    source_permissions => 'ignore',
  }
  file { 'c:/windows/temp/helloworld':
    ensure             => 'directory',
    source_permissions => 'ignore',
  }
}
```

In the preceding manifest, we referred to the new template that we have just created. Now we come to testing. Here are the details of `hello.txt` after a test run:

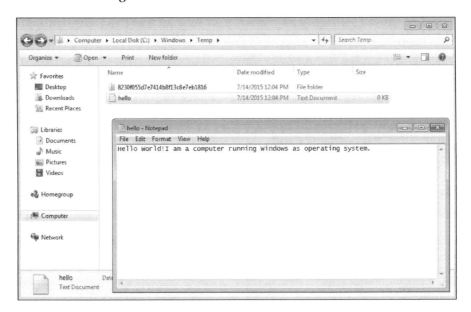

As we can see, it has correctly written the operating system as `Windows`. However, there is a tiny problem. The Linux file format and the Windows file format have different line endings. We can correct this by adding `<%= "\r\n" %>`. Here is the new template file that will also put the line feeds:

After running the Puppet test again, here are the file details:

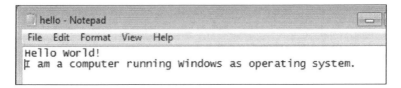

Now, we also have the correct line feeds. In the next topic, we will use templates to solve a more advanced problem.

An example template to edit the registry keys

Now, we will start a more advanced example. In this example, we will use FortiClient SSLVPN. You can install it manually to complete this example. You can download the file from `http://hacktr.org/download/forticlient-sslvpn/`.

Assume that you are using FortiGate as a firewall in your company. You are installing the SSLVPN client on all of your user computers and also need to define the connection details. You want to automate the installation and connection definition. There are hundreds of computers in different locations. Completing all of these installations and connection definitions may lead to a good amount of work for the helpdesk, if they are not automated. (We will tell you how to install the software with Puppet in the final chapter.)

Following is the screenshot of FortiClient SSLVPN after its initial installation. As we can see, there is no connection definition:

Now let's add a new connection detail from **Settings**. In the new window, click the **New Connection** button to add the details:

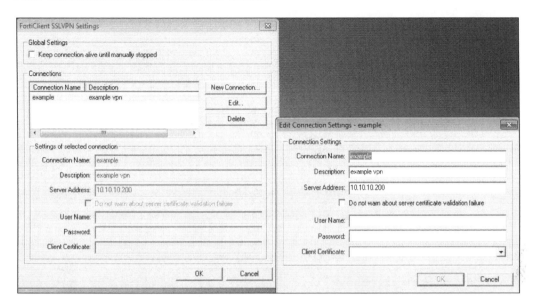

In the preceding screenshot, you can see the sample details. After adding the details, we can search these details in the registry and learn where to add the values. Navigate to start menu, **Run** and run regedit.exe. Search for the text with the description example vpn. The first search brings the HKEY_CURRENT_USER details. This is not useful and we need to search more, wherever the changes are made under an SID.

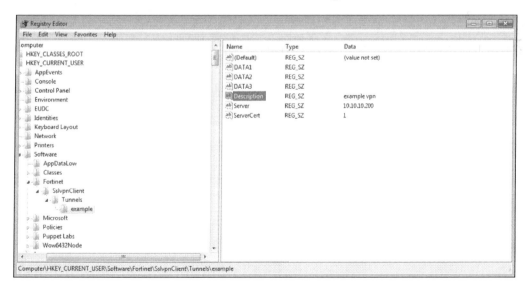

The following is the correct entry. This entry is under HKEY_USERS and under an SID. We will define the connection detail for each user. So the full path is HKEY_USERS\ [SID]\Software\Fortinet\SslvpnClient\Tunnels\. SID is the variable and will change for each user.

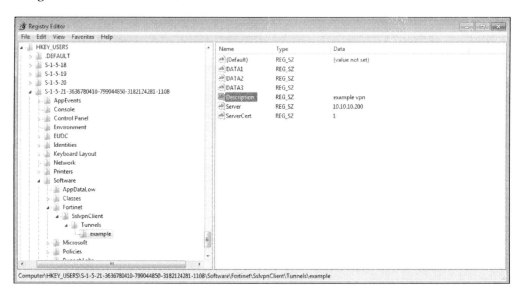

Now right-click the example key on the left-hand side and export the key. We will check its details and understand how to write a registry entry correctly. The exported .reg file details are shown as follows:

Now we have enough details to write our template and define the connection details for all the users. We will create a module named `fortivpn`. Its structure is given as follows:

```
root@puppetmaster:/etc/puppet/modules# tree fortivpn/
fortivpn/
├── manifests
│   └── init.pp
└── templates
    └── forti.erb

2 directories, 2 files
root@puppetmaster:/etc/puppet/modules# ▓
```

Here are the template details:

```
 1 Windows Registry Editor Version 5.00
 2
 3 <%
 4 sids = @sids.split(',')
 5 sids.each do |sid|
 6
 7 %>
 8 [-HKEY_USERS\<%= sid %>\Software\Fortinet\SslvpnClient\Tunnels]
 9 [HKEY_USERS\<%= sid %>\Software\Fortinet\SslvpnClient\Tunnels\examplesslvpn]
10
11 "Description"="EXAMPLE SSLVPN"
12 "Server"="10.10.10.200:10443"
13 "ServerCert"="1"
14
15 <%
16 end
17 %>
```

Now let's see what we have done at the `each` line `sids = @sids.split(',')`.

As you will remember, we defined the `sids` fact before and now we are using it as `@sids`. We added each SID in the comma delimited format. Now we can split the values and assign them to a variable in an array format. We accomplish this by the `"split(',')` command:

```
"sids.each do |sid|":
```

Here, we loop for each value of `sids` and assign it to the `sid` variable. At line **8**, we delete the entries that may exist. Between lines **9** and **13**, we define the new values. Line **16** ends the loop.

We will create a `.reg` file from this template. With the `.reg` file, we will update the registry using the `exec` resource and execute `regedit.exe /s registryfile.erb`. Now, let's switch to our manifest.

```
 1 # Add fortivpn connection details to registry
 2 class fortivpn {
 3   file { 'c:/windows/temp/fortissl.reg':
 4     content           => template('fortivpn/forti.erb'),
 5     source_permissions => 'ignore',
 6   }
 7
 8   exec { 'addregistry':
 9     command     => 'Regedit.exe /s C:\\Windows\\Temp\\fortissl.reg',
10     path        => 'C:/Windows',
11     subscribe   => File['c:/windows/temp/fortissl.reg'],
12     refreshonly => true,
13   }
14 }
```

As you can see from the preceding screenshot, we are creating a new file from the `forti.erb` template from lines **3** to **6**. After this, the `regedit.exe` command is executed. The `exec` resource will run only if the `fortissl.reg` file is changed. This is done by subscribing to the file at line **11**.

First, we import the module into Foreman and assign it to the host. We will not mention this repeatedly after creating each module. As a rule of thumb, if we create a new module and want to test it, we have to import it and assign it to a host.

The following are the test run details:

```
C:\Users\puppet1>puppet agent --test
Info: Retrieving pluginfacts
Info: Retrieving plugin
Info: Loading facts
Info: Caching catalog for windowstest.example.local
Info: Applying configuration version '1431106969'
Notice: /Stage[main]/Fortivpn/File[c:/windows/temp/fortissl.reg]/ensure: defined
 content as '{md5}52633d5464e39baa694291fae8317783'
Info: /Stage[main]/Fortivpn/File[c:/windows/temp/fortissl.reg]: Scheduling refre
sh of Exec[addregistry]
Notice: /Stage[main]/Fortivpn/Exec[addregistry]: Triggered 'refresh' from 1 even
ts
Notice: Finished catalog run in 1.16 seconds

C:\Users\puppet1>
```

After the test run, here are the details in FortiClient SSLVPN:

 As you can see, we do not need to stick to only one solution. We have the option to use the registry module from Puppet Forge or we can execute the changes by a command.

The Puppet functions

Functions are predefined codes of Ruby. For example, the `template('modulename/templatename')` code we used in the templates example is a function that is calling the template file as content. Most of the functions return a value or modify the catalog. In the next section, we will start with the `stdlib` functions.

The stdlib functions

There are many ready-made functions in the `stdlib` module. The complete module name is `puppetlabs-stdlib`. As the module name implies, the `stdlib` module has many standard definitions that can be used in different modules. In this section, we will just see some of the function examples and how to use them. You can find the full reference from `https://forge.puppetlabs.com/puppetlabs/stdlib`. To install the module, use the following command in the Puppet Master terminal:

```
$ sudo puppet module install puppetlabs-stdlib
```

For the following examples, we will create a sample module named `testfunctions`. The module will not do anything at all but will display the results of the tested functions. The following is the structure of our module:

```
root@puppetmaster:/etc/puppet/modules# tree testfunctions/
testfunctions/
└── manifests
    └── init.pp

1 directory, 1 file
root@puppetmaster:/etc/puppet/modules# 
```

Some string functions – downcase, upcase, and capitalize

The names of the following functions already imply what they do:

- `downcase`: This returns the given text in lowercase
- `upcase`: This returns the given text in uppercase
- `capitalize`: This capitalizes the first letter of the given text

Following is our sample code:

```
# just testing some stdlib functions
classtestfunctions {
$strvar1 = 'tHis IS A text.'
notify { "This is the default text: ${strvar1}":}

$strup1 = upcase($strvar1)
notify { "This is the upcase function output: ${strup1}":}

$strdown1 = downcase($strvar1)
notify { "This is the downcase function output: ${strdown1}":}

$strcap1 = capitalize($strvar1)
notify { "This is the capitalize function output: ${strcap1}":}
}
```

In the previous text, we defined different variables such as `strvar1`, `strup1`, `strdown1`, and `strcap1`. As you can see, we changed the details of `strvar1` for each variable with a function and we displayed the results with `notify`. Following is the output of the module test run:

```
C:\Users\puppet1>puppet agent --test
Info: Retrieving pluginfacts
Info: Retrieving plugin
Info: Loading facts
Info: Caching catalog for windowstest.example.local
Info: Applying configuration version '1431114521'
Notice: This is the upcase function output: THIS IS A TEXT.
Notice: /Stage[main]/Testfunctions/Notify[This is the upcase function output: TH
IS IS A TEXT.]/message: defined 'message' as 'This is the upcase function output
: THIS IS A TEXT.'
Notice: This is the downcase function output: this is a text.
Notice: /Stage[main]/Testfunctions/Notify[This is the downcase function output:
this is a text.]/message: defined 'message' as 'This is the downcase function ou
tput: this is a text.'
Notice: This is the default text: tHis IS A text.
Notice: /Stage[main]/Testfunctions/Notify[This is the default text: tHis IS A te
xt.]/message: defined 'message' as 'This is the default text: tHis IS A text.'
Notice: This is the capitalize function output: This is a text.
Notice: /Stage[main]/Testfunctions/Notify[This is the capitalize function output
: This is a text.]/message: defined 'message' as 'This is the capitalize functio
n output: This is a text.'
Notice: Finished catalog run in 0.14 seconds

C:\Users\puppet1>
```

 As you can see, the output is not in an ordered fashion and according to our manifest. This is because the manifests are not processed in this way. If you need an order, you have to define it clearly with the `require` parameter.

The pw_hash function

This function hashes a password. It needs three parameters. First one is the password text, second is the hash type (possible values: MD5, SHA-256, and SHA-512), and the third value is the salt.

In the following example, to make the output clear, we are commenting the other function codes:

```
# just testing some stdlib functions
class testfunctions {
  $strvar1 = 'tHis IS A text.'
# notify { "This is the default text: ${strvar1}":}

# $strup1 = upcase($strvar1)
# notify { "This is the upcase function output: ${strup1}":}

# $strdown1 = downcase($strvar1)
# notify { "This is the downcase function output: ${strdown1}":}

# $strcap1 = capitalize($strvar1)
# notify { "This is the capitalize function output: ${strcap1}":}

  $strpass1 = pw_hash($strvar1,'SHA-512','salty')
  notify { "This is the pw_hash function output: ${strpass1}":}
}
```

Following is the test run results:

```
root@puppetmaster:/etc/puppet/modules# puppet agent --test
Info: Retrieving pluginfacts
Info: Retrieving plugin
Info: Loading facts
Info: Caching catalog for puppetmaster.example.com
Info: Applying configuration version '1431120361'
Notice: This is the pw_hash function output: $6$salty$TKydTsfbXrDHQG77yG2gYehvqWLTAD5AEaLsYhNOfZo.hJFy17j/mpUjY
500Z.FkpVHCSQLWLS3Sb/amo1Hxk/
Notice: /Stage[main]/Testfunctions/Notify[This is the pw_hash function output: $6$salty$TKydTsfbXrDHQG77yG2gYeh
vqWLTAD5AEaLsYhNOfZo.hJFy17j/mpUjY500Z.FkpVHCSQLWLS3Sb/amo1Hxk/]/message: defined 'message' as 'This is the pw_
hash function output: $6$salty$TKydTsfbXrDHQG77yG2gYehvqWLTAD5AEaLsYhNOfZo.hJFy17j/mpUjY500Z.FkpVHCSQLWLS3Sb/am
o1Hxk/'
Notice: Finished catalog run in 0.19 seconds
```

The purpose of this topic was to show you how to use functions and show some example functions in stdlib. If you need more functions, first please check out the stdlib functions. If you cannot find the relevant function, it is time to write your own function.

Your first function

After learning about the functions, it is time to create your own function. To create your function, first of all, you need to install the stdlib module. We installed it in the previous section, so we can start writing our custom function.

To create our new function, we need to create a myfirstfunction.rb file under the stdlib/lib/puppet/parser/functions stdlib module. Here is a simple code:

```
module Puppet::Parser::Functions
newfunction(
:myfirstfunction,
:type => :rvalue,
```

```
:doc => "Testing the first function. ") do |args|
value = args[0]
result = "Hello World Function: " + value
return result
end
end
```

As you can see in the preceding code, this is a very simple function. Now let's explain each line. Following is a screenshot with the line numbers:

```
 1 module Puppet::Parser::Functions
 2   newfunction(
 3     :myfirstfunction,
 4     :type => :rvalue,
 5     :doc => "Testing the first function. ") do |args|
 6     value = args[0]
 7     result = "Hello World Function: " + value
 8     return result
 9   end
10 end
```

The file name for this function is myfirstfunction.rb. You should think of the first two lines and the last line as prerequisites to write the function.

- **Line 3**: The function name.
- **Line 4**: The type of the function. It says that the function will return a value.
- **Line 5**: :doc is the text documentation of function. do |args| is to get the input parameters of the function.
- **Line 6**: This gets the first parameter of the function and assigns it to the value variable. You can use more than one parameter such as args[0], args[1].
- **Line 7**: This concatenates the value with the Hello World Function: text and assigns it to the result variable.
- **Line 8**: This returns the result variable as a function output.

Again, we will use our test functions module and will add the following lines:

```
$strtest1 = myfirstfunction('test123')
notify { "This is the myfirstfunction function output: ${strtest1}":}
```

Here are the results of the test run:

```
 1 module Puppet::Parser::Functions
 2   newfunction(
 3     :myfirstfunction,
 4     :type => :rvalue,
 5     :doc => "Testing the first function. ") do |args|
 6     value = args[0]
 7     result = "Hello World Function: " + value
 8     return result
 9   end
10 end
```

This function was just a simple example. From now on, you can create any function with complex details. In the security section later, we will create our own function that will create different passwords for the local admin user of each host.

Summary

In this chapter, we learned many advanced topics. We started off with facts. In Puppet facts, we learned how to display them and checked out a few standard facts that are already defined. After this, we created our own facts. Another topic was the templates to create dynamic content files. We used a template to create some registry entries for each user in Windows. Then, we finally rounded off with functions. We learned the stdlib functions and how to call them in the manifests. Finally, we created our own simple custom function and used it in a manifest.

In the next chapter, we will see how we can use Puppet to secure our hosts and put them in a desired state.

6
Using Puppet for Windows Security

Let's do a quick recap of what we have learned until now. We learned how to write modules, facts, templates, and functions. We learned how to deal with files and the firewall, execute commands, and many such details. Now, we will bring them all together and use them for the following security practices:

- Locking the Startup folder for each user
- Locking the hosts file
- Stopping unnecessary services
- Making sure that the necessary services are running
- Denying incoming traffic and allowing only the necessary ports
- Making the local administrator password unique

For each topic, we will also address why we need these settings. The best thing with Puppet is that when you make a security setting, it cannot be undone. If somebody changes the settings, Puppet will correct it in the next run (the default interval is 30 minutes).

Locking the Startup folder

Normally, each user in Windows can change the contents of the Startup folder. The Startup folder items are executed when the user is logged in. A hacker can enter his code here, so that after each restart his code can run again and connect to the command and control centre. To prevent this, we will lock every user's Startup folder.

The full path of the `Startup` folder for a user is `C:\Users\puppet1\AppData\Roaming\Microsoft\Windows\Start Menu\Programs\Startup`. This is also shown in the following screenshot:

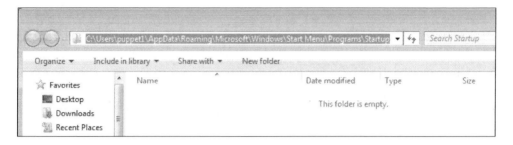

The permission details are as described in the following screenshot. As we can see, the user has full control:

To change all the users' `Startup` folder permissions, we need to know the IDs of the users. As you will remember, we have already defined the users as a fact in *Chapter 5, Puppet Facts, Functions, and Templates,* in the *Adding Windows users as custom facts* section topic. In addition to this, we need to use the ACL module that we mentioned in *Chapter 4, Puppet Forge Modules for Windows* in *The access control list* section.

In this example, we are creating a new module named `lockstartup`. Following are the details of the code:

```
1 # locks startup folder
2 class lockstartup {
3
4   $array_users = split($::users, ',')
5
6 # this type locks the user startup folder
7   define winstartupfolder {
8     $user = $name
9     acl {"c:/Users/${user}/AppData/Roaming/Microsoft/Windows/Start Menu/Programs/Startup":
10      purge                   => true,
11      permissions             => [
12        { identity => 'SYSTEM', rights => ['full'], child_types => 'all' },
13        { identity => 'ADMINISTRATORS', rights => ['full'], child_types => 'all' },
14        { identity => 'Authenticated Users', rights => ['read','execute'] },
15      ],
16      inherit_parent_permissions => false,
17    }
18  }
19
20  winstartupfolder { $array_users:; }
21 }
```

Here are the details of each line:

Line 4:

Here, we are getting the values of the `users` fact and putting the values in an `$array_users` array variable. Remember that we defined the users fact in *Chapter 5, Puppet Facts, Functions, and Templates*. The array variable does not have to start with the `array` keyword, we can give any name to it.

Line 7:

Here, we have defined a new type. This type will work for each of the array values that we send. The basic usage is as follows:

```
definetypename {
    $Inputvariable = $name

    ....
}
```

The input can be used with the `$name` variable. We can call the type multiple times using the following code as required:

```
typename { $anarray:; }
```

This code will call the type for each value of the array. Even though a loop command is not available in the manifests, it is possible to execute the same code for each array value.

Lines between 10-17:

These are the lines that are calling the `acl`. We are setting the full control for the SYSTEM, and ADMINISTRATORS All `Authenticated Users` will have `read` and `execute` rights. Line 10 ensures that all the permissions are purged, so that only the permissions we enable will be available.

Line 20:

This calls the new defined type for each value in the array.

Now, it is time to test the module. The results of the test run are shown in the following screenshot:

As we can see in the preceding screenshot, the code runs without any problems for the users except the `Administrator` user. So, what is the problem with the `Administrator` user? This happens when there is a user who has never logged in. However, he or she has executed some command with his or her credentials. In this case, Windows creates the `user` folder and the SID details in the registry. However, the problem is that the `Startup` folder will not be created if the user does not log in. The following screenshot shows that the `Startup` folder does not exist for the `Administrator` user.

So, this error is not a problem:

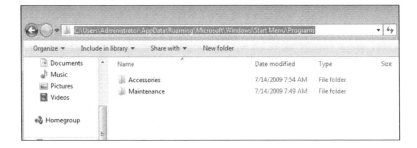

Now, let's check the permissions of a user. As we can see in the following screenshot, only the users that we have defined are present and **Authenticated Users** do not have full control:

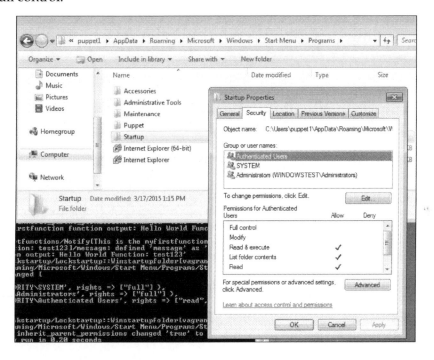

Locking the hosts file

The `hosts` file is the file that Windows uses to resolve any domain names before confirming with a nameserver. Let's assume that your favorite bank's IP is changed in that file and when you try to do some transactions you open a cloned version of your bank's website. You assume that it is the legitimate site because you see the name correctly displayed in the address bar.

Normally, the `hosts` file can be changed only by administrators. However, we want to ensure that it cannot be changed even by administrator accounts and is always same in all the hosts. Achieving this is very easy with Puppet. We will only upload our ideal copy of the `hosts` file to Puppet Master under a module and with a file resource we will maintain it in all of our hosts.

In the following screenshot, you can see the full path of the `hosts` file:

```
C:\Windows\System32\+drivers\etc
```

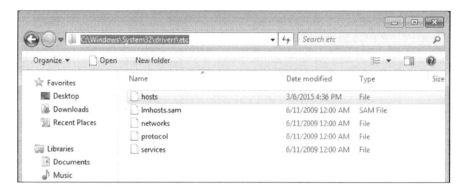

The following items are contained in a `hosts` file. In this example, as we do not own the `example.com` domain, the IP of `puppetmaster.example.com` is here with a local IP. Now, assume that there is another IP and domain to collect your bank information or any other important information.

```
# Copyright (c) 1993-2009 Microsoft Corp.
#
# This is a sample HOSTS file used by Microsoft TCP/IP for Windows.
#
# This file contains the mappings of IP addresses to host names. Each
# entry should be kept on an individual line. The IP address should
# be placed in the first column followed by the corresponding host name.
# The IP address and the host name should be separated by at least one
# space.
#
# Additionally, comments (such as these) may be inserted on individual
# lines or following the machine name denoted by a '#' symbol.
#
# For example:
#
#      102.54.94.97     rhino.acme.com          # source server
#       38.25.63.10     x.acme.com              # x client host

# localhost name resolution is handled within DNS itself.
#       127.0.0.1       localhost
#       ::1             localhost
10.10.10.10 puppetmaster.example.com
```

We will just insert another line with a comment in the last line informing that it is locked by `puppetmaster`, as shown in the following code snippet:

```
# Locked by Puppetmaster. Do not change. All of the changes will be
overwritten.
```

After adding these details to the last line, we will insert this file into our module. The module name will be `lockhostsfile` and the following screenshot shows the module structure:

```
lockhostsfile/
├── files
│   └── hosts
└── manifests
    └── init.pp

2 directories, 2 files
root@puppetmaster:/etc/puppet/modules# ▌
```

The manifest details are shown in the following screenshot. As we can see, it is a very simple manifest with only one *file resource*:

```
# lock the hosts file
class lockhostsfile {
  file { 'C:/Windows/System32/drivers/etc/hosts':
    source             => 'puppet:///modules/lockhostsfile/hosts',
    source_permissions => 'ignore',
  }
}
```

We can see the output, as shown in the following screenshot, when we run the Puppet agent:

```
C:\Users\puppet1>puppet agent --test
Info: Retrieving pluginfacts
Info: Retrieving plugin
Info: Loading facts
Info: Caching catalog for windowstest.example.local
Info: Applying configuration version '1431129990'
Notice: /Stage[main]/Lockhostsfile/File[C:/Windows/System32/drivers/etc/hosts]/c
ontent:

Info: Computing checksum on file C:/Windows/System32/drivers/etc/hosts
Info: /Stage[main]/Lockhostsfile/File[C:/Windows/System32/drivers/etc/hosts]: Fi
lebucketed C:/Windows/System32/drivers/etc/hosts to puppet with sum 78850af45319
6d6ce2f0bcfffcd13df9
Notice: /Stage[main]/Lockhostsfile/File[C:/Windows/System32/drivers/etc/hosts]/c
ontent: content changed '{md5}78850af453196d6ce2f0bcfffcd13df9' to '{md5}56c0e67
3f7e9008684cae41bc4d2e92e'
Notice: Finished catalog run in 0.38 seconds

C:\Users\puppet1>
```

The following screenshot shows the details of the `hosts` file after a test run:

```
# Copyright (c) 1993-2009 Microsoft Corp.
#
# This is a sample HOSTS file used by Microsoft TCP/IP for Windows.
#
# This file contains the mappings of IP addresses to host names. Each
# entry should be kept on an individual line. The IP address should
# be placed in the first column followed by the corresponding host name.
# The IP address and the host name should be separated by at least one
# space.
#
# Additionally, comments (such as these) may be inserted on individual
# lines or following the machine name denoted by a '#' symbol.
#
# For example:
#
#      102.54.94.97     rhino.acme.com          # source server
#       38.25.63.10     x.acme.com              # x client host

# localhost name resolution is handled within DNS itself.
#       127.0.0.1       localhost
#       ::1             localhost
10.10.10.10 puppetmaster.example.com
# Locked by Puppetmaster. Do not change. All of the changes will be overwritten.
```

As a test run, you can change the contents of the hosts file or even delete it. It will be back with its contents in the next run.

Stopping unnecessary services

In this section, we will stop the services that we do not use frequently. In the *Managing services* section under *Chapter 3, Your First Modules*, we already stopped the SMB service for file and printer sharing. For users, we do not want them to share the folders and printers directly. All the sharing must be achieved through the file server or the document management system. Also, leaving these services open gives more opportunities to hackers to understand and footprint the target system. When we disable the SMB service, the hackers cannot exploit them.

We will create a module named `stopservices`. It will have a very basic structure and will only have an `init.pp` file. The structure is shown in the following screenshot:

```
stopservices/
└── manifests
    └── init.pp

1 directory, 1 file
root@puppetmaster:/etc/puppet/modules#
```

First, let's copy and paste the code we used previously:

```
# stop unnecessary services
class stopservices {

# stop SMB
  service { 'Browser':
    ensure  => stopped,
    enable  => false,
  }

  service { 'LanmanServer':
    ensure  => stopped,
    enable  => false,
    require => Service['Browser'],
  }
}
```

In the next step, we will also disable **Remote Desktop Services** for clients. We can do this only if we use a remote desktop management solution. Most corporations have this, so it becomes unnecessary to use RDP at the same time. Let's check its details. The following screenshot shows the RDP services. We need to stop the selected services. First, we need to stop **Remote Desktop Services UserMode Port Redirector** (UmRdpService) and after this, **Remote Desktop Services** (TermService):

Software Protection	Enables the download, installation and enforcement...	Started	Automatic	Network S...
Certificate Propagation	Copies user certificates and root certificates from s...	Started	Manual	Local Syste...
Remote Desktop Configuration	Remote Desktop Configuration service (RDCS) is res...	Started	Manual	Local Syste...
Remote Desktop Services	Allows users to connect interactively to a remote co...	Started	Manual	Network S...
Remote Desktop Services UserMode ...	Allows the redirection of Printers/Drives/Ports for R...	Started	Manual	Local Syste...
ActiveX Installer (AxInstSV)	Provides User Account Control validation for the ins...		Manual	Local Syste...
Adaptive Brightness	Monitors ambient light sensors to detect changes in...		Manual	Local Service

After adding these details, our manifest appears as shown in the following screenshot. In the manifest, we have also added the service display names for easy reference:

```
# stop unnecessary services
class stopservices {

# stop SMB
# service display name "Computer Browser"
  service { 'Browser':
    ensure  => stopped,
    enable  => false,
  }
# service display name "Server"
  service { 'LanmanServer':
    ensure  => stopped,
    enable  => false,
    require => Service['Browser'],
  }

# stop Remote Desktop Service
# service display name "Remote Desktop Services UserMode Port Redirector"
  service { 'UmRdpService':
    ensure  => stopped,
    enable  => false,
  }
# service display name "Remote Desktop Services"
  service { 'TermService':
    ensure  => stopped,
    enable  => false,
    require => Service['UmRdpService'],
  }
}
```

The following screenshot shows the test run details:

```
C:\Users\puppet1>puppet agent --test
Info: Retrieving pluginfacts
Info: Retrieving plugin
Info: Loading facts
Info: Caching catalog for windowstest.example.local
Info: Applying configuration version '1432555427'
Notice: /Stage[main]/Stopservices/Service[UmRdpService]/ensure: ensure changed '
running' to 'stopped'
Notice: /Stage[main]/Stopservices/Service[TermService]/ensure: ensure changed 'r
unning' to 'stopped'
Notice: Finished catalog run in 6.23 seconds

C:\Users\puppet1>
```

We may not disable SMB and RDP on the server side. However, after disabling SMB and RDP on the client computers, the hackers will have a really hard time attacking them.

Making sure that the security-related services are running

After stopping the unnecessary services, the next step is to start any stopped services that are required. The most important security services for us are the firewall and antivirus services. The steps in this section are really specific to each enterprise; you could be using the Windows Firewall or any antivirus firewall. Also, you could have different options for the antivirus software. Here, we assume that you are using the Windows Firewall and Trend Micro antivirus software.

If you want to test the same scenario you may download **Trend Micro Antivirus+ 2015** from http://downloadcenter.trendmicro.com/.

Most of the time, the new generation antivirus software protect their services and tasks. So stopping the services of an antivirus may not be an easy task. You may use Process Hacker (http://processhacker.sourceforge.net/index.php) to do this.

The following screenshot assures us that the antivirus is running properly:

The following screenshot shows the processes for Trend Micro in Process Hacker. We will terminate all of them from Process Hacker. You need to have administrator rights to do this:

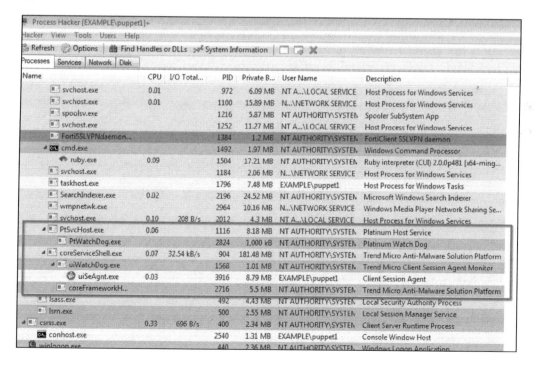

The services details are shown in the following screenshot:

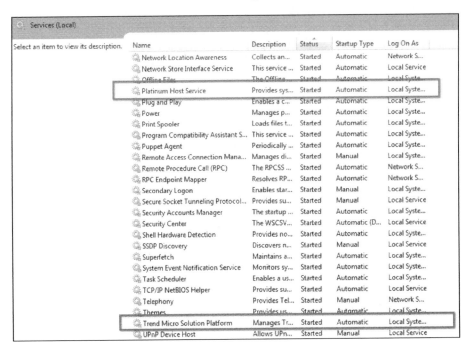

We will check the following two services: **Platinum Host Service** (`Platinum Host Service`) and **Trend Micro Solution Platform** (`Amsp`). So let's start writing our manifest. The module name will be `startservices`. Here are the structure details:

```
stopservices/
└── manifests
    └── init.pp

1 directory, 1 file
root@puppetmaster:/etc/puppet/modules#
```

As we know the service names, now we can write the manifest details:

```
# start necessary services
class startservices {

# start Trendmicro antivirus
  service { 'Amsp':
    ensure => running,
    enable => true,
  }

  service { 'Platinum Host Service':
    ensure => running,
    enable => true,
  }
}
```

The following screenshot shows the test run details:

```
C:\Users\puppet1>puppet agent --test
Info: Retrieving pluginfacts
Info: Retrieving plugin
Info: Loading facts
Info: Caching catalog for windowstest.example.local
Info: Applying configuration version '1432640813'
Notice: /Stage[main]/Startservices/Service[Amsp]/ensure: ensure changed 'stopped
' to 'running'
Info: /Stage[main]/Startservices/Service[Amsp]: Unscheduling refresh on Service[
Amsp]
Notice: /Stage[main]/Startservices/Service[Platinum Host Service]/ensure: ensure
 changed 'stopped' to 'running'
Info: /Stage[main]/Startservices/Service[Platinum Host Service]: Unscheduling re
fresh on Service[Platinum Host Service]
Notice: Finished catalog run in 8.23 seconds

C:\Users\puppet1>
```

As we can see in the preceding screenshot, the services for Trend Micro have started again.

Now, we can also include the Windows Firewall service in our list. The name for this is MpsSvc. The following screenshot shows the details of the manifest after including Windows Firewall:

```
# start necessary services
class startservices  {

# start Trendmicro antivirus
  service { 'Amsp':
    ensure  => running,
    enable  => true,
  }

  service { 'Platinum Host Service':
    ensure  => running,
    enable  => true,
  }

# start Windows Firewall
  service { 'MpsSvc':
    ensure  => running,
    enable  => true,
  }
}
```

While testing, you can first manually stop the firewall service to see if it starts again. The test run results are shown in the following screenshot:

```
C:\Users\puppet1>puppet agent --test
Info: Retrieving pluginfacts
Info: Retrieving plugin
Info: Loading facts
Info: Caching catalog for windowstest.example.local
Info: Applying configuration version '1432650847'
Notice: /Stage[main]/Startservices/Service[MpsSvc]/ensure: ensure changed 'stopp
ed' to 'running'
Info: /Stage[main]/Startservices/Service[MpsSvc]: Unscheduling refresh on Servic
e[MpsSvc]
Notice: Finished catalog run in 3.25 seconds

C:\Users\puppet1>
```

Here, a last point to note is that you can include any service in this example. For example, it will be a good idea to add any backup services and update services in this manifest.

Denying all incoming traffic and allowing only the necessary ports

We will first ensure that the firewall is running. After this, we will apply some rules to enable some ports and disable others.

To ensure that the firewall is running, we need to first ensure that the profiles are enabled and second, the firewall service is enabled and running. We have already mentioned how to enable firewall profiles in the topic *Chapter 4, Puppet Forge Modules for Windows* in the *Managing the registry* section. The following screenshot shows the code from that section.

```
# enable windows firewall profiles
class firewallon {
  registry::value { 'firewalldomain':
    key   => 'HKLM\SYSTEM\CurrentControlSet\Services\SharedAccess\Parameters\FirewallPolicy\DomainProfile',
    value => 'EnableFirewall',
    type  => 'dword',
    data  => '1',
  }

  registry::value { 'firewallstandard':
    key   => 'HKLM\SYSTEM\CurrentControlSet\Services\SharedAccess\Parameters\FirewallPolicy\StandardProfile',
    value => 'EnableFirewall',
    type  => 'dword',
    data  => '1',
  }

  registry::value { 'firewallpublic':
    key   => 'HKLM\SYSTEM\CurrentControlSet\Services\SharedAccess\Parameters\FirewallPolicy\PublicProfile',
    value => 'EnableFirewall',
    type  => 'dword',
    data  => '1',
  }
}
```

For the changes to take effect, we restart the firewall service. For this purpose, the firewall service will be notified for each registry change. Thus, whenever one of the profiles is changed from `disabled` to `enabled`, the firewall service will restart to activate the changes.

The new module name is `winfirewall` and the following screenshot shows its structure:

```
root@puppetmaster:/etc/puppet/modules# tree winfirewall
winfirewall
└── manifests
    └── init.pp

1 directory, 1 file
root@puppetmaster:/etc/puppet/modules# []
```

The following screenshot shows the details after the inclusion of the service details. You can see that the service details are commented. We have already defined this service in the `stopservices` module. Thus, defining it again will give an error. You can directly refer to a definition in another module. You only need to ensure that the module you refer to is active and assigned to the host or host group:

```
# windows firewall enable and add rules
class winfirewall {

  if $::osfamily == 'windows' {
    registry::value { 'firewalldomain':
      key     => 'HKLM\SYSTEM\CurrentControlSet\Services\SharedAccess\Parameters\FirewallPolicy\DomainProfile',
      value   => 'EnableFirewall',
      type    => 'dword',
      data    => '1',
      notify  => Service['MpsSvc'],
    }

    registry::value { 'firewallstandard':
      key     => 'HKLM\SYSTEM\CurrentControlSet\Services\SharedAccess\Parameters\FirewallPolicy\StandardProfile',
      value   => 'EnableFirewall',
      type    => 'dword',
      data    => '1',
      notify  => Service['MpsSvc'],
    }

    registry::value { 'firewallpublic':
      key     => 'HKLM\SYSTEM\CurrentControlSet\Services\SharedAccess\Parameters\FirewallPolicy\PublicProfile',
      value   => 'EnableFirewall',
      type    => 'dword',
      data    => '1',
      notify  => Service['MpsSvc'],
    }
# start Windows Firewall - Already defined in startservices so we will not define here
#   service { 'MpsSvc':
#     ensure  => running,
#     enable  => true,
#   }

  } else {
    notify {"This module runs only for Windows OS family. This host has OS family $::osfamily":}
  }
}
```

Now, let's see the test results. In our example, the `domain` and `public` profiles are disabled and the firewall service is stopped.

Be careful about defining a resource with the same name in different modules. If you have the same names, it will give a duplicate error. In our example, we have a registry value change named `firewalldomain` in the `winfirewall` class and also in the `firewallon` class. While assigning `firewalldomain` to your hosts, please remove the `firewallon` class. The new class that we have defined is more detailed, and the other class is not needed anymore.

```
C:\Users\puppet1>puppet agent --test
Info: Retrieving pluginfacts
Info: Retrieving plugin
Info: Loading facts
Info: Caching catalog for windowstest.example.local
Info: Applying configuration version '1432656557'
Notice: /Stage[main]/Winfirewall/Registry::Value[firewalldomain]/Registry_value[
HKLM\SYSTEM\CurrentControlSet\Services\SharedAccess\Parameters\FirewallPolicy\Do
mainProfile\EnableFirewall]/data: data changed '0' to '1'
Info: Registry::Value[firewalldomain]: Scheduling refresh of Service[MpsSvc]
Notice: /Stage[main]/Winfirewall/Registry::Value[firewallpublic]/Registry_value[
HKLM\SYSTEM\CurrentControlSet\Services\SharedAccess\Parameters\FirewallPolicy\Pu
blicProfile\EnableFirewall]/data: data changed '0' to '1'
Info: Registry::Value[firewallpublic]: Scheduling refresh of Service[MpsSvc]
Notice: /Stage[main]/Startservices/Service[MpsSvc]/ensure: ensure changed 'stopp
ed' to 'running'
Info: /Stage[main]/Startservices/Service[MpsSvc]: Unscheduling refresh on Servic
e[MpsSvc]
Notice: Finished catalog run in 3.30 seconds

C:\Users\puppet1>
```

As we can see in the previous screenshot, the profiles are enabled and the firewall service has been restarted.

Our next step is to check the firewall rules. By default, if there are no rules, the inbound connections are denied in the Windows Firewall. The details can be seen in the following screenshot:

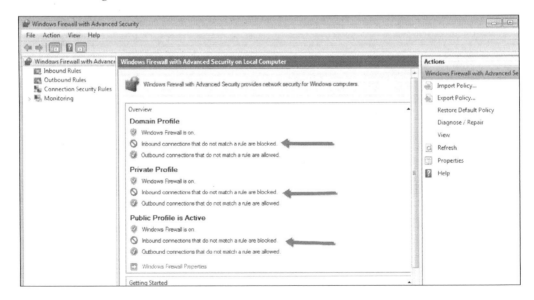

However, there are default rules that enable the SMB and RDP ports in the profiles. So, we need to find and delete, or disable them. As they are default rules, disabling them may be a better option than deleting them. The following screenshot shows the default RDP inbound rule:

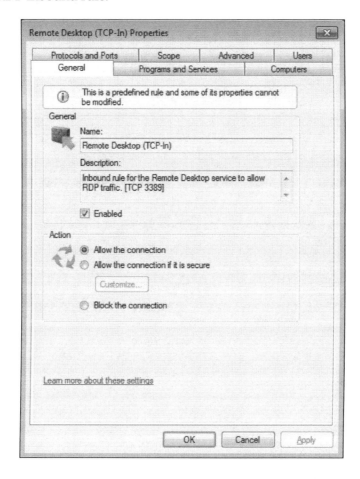

To disable this rule, we will use the `netsh` command that works in Command Prompt. We are not using the unsupported firewall module, as the results are not satisfactory. The command to disable the rule is as follows:

```
C:\>netshadvfirewall firewall set rule name="Remote Desktop (TCP-In)" new enable=no
```

Also, we want to deny all the traffic for the 445 port. Checking the default settings in the rules, we can see in the following screenshot that **File and Printer Sharing (SMB-In)** is enabled. So, we will disable this too:

BranchCache Hosted Cache Server (HTT...	BranchCache - Hosted Cache Server (Uses ...	All	TCP	443	No	Allow	N	
Secure Socket Tunneling Protocol (SSTP-...	Secure Socket Tunneling Protocol	All	TCP	443	No	Allow	N	
File and Printer Sharing (SMB-In)	File and Printer Sharing	Domain	TCP	445	No	Allow	N	
File and Printer Sharing (SMB-In)	File and Printer Sharing	Public	TCP	445	No	Allow	N	
File and Printer Sharing (SMB-In)	File and Printer Sharing	Private	TCP	445	Yes	Allow	N	
Netlogon Service (NP-In)	Netlogon Service	All	TCP	445	No	Allow	N	
Remote Event Log Management (NP-In)	Remote Event Log Management	Private...	TCP	445	No	Allow	N	
Remote Event Log Management (NP-In)	Remote Event Log Management	Domain	TCP	445	No	Allow	N	
Remote Service Management (NP-In)	Remote Service Management	Private...	TCP	445	No	Allow	N	
Remote Service Management (NP-In)	Remote Service Management	Domain	TCP	445	No	Allow	N	
File and Printer Sharing (LLMNR-UDP-In)	File and Printer Sharing	Domai...	UDP	5355	No	Allow	N	

The following command disables this rule for all the profiles:

```
C:\>netshadvfirewall firewall set rule name="File and Printer Sharing
(SMB-In)" new enable=no
```

After learning these details, we update our manifest and the details are shown in the following screenshot:

```
# windows firewall enable and add rules
class winfirewall {

  if $::osfamily == 'windows' {
    registry::value { 'firewalldomain':
      key    => 'HKLM\SYSTEM\CurrentControlSet\Services\SharedAccess\Parameters\FirewallPolicy\DomainProfile',
      value  => 'EnableFirewall',
      type   => 'dword',
      data   => '1',
      notify => Service['MpsSvc'],
    }

    registry::value { 'firewallstandard':
      key    => 'HKLM\SYSTEM\CurrentControlSet\Services\SharedAccess\Parameters\FirewallPolicy\StandardProfile',
      value  => 'EnableFirewall',
      type   => 'dword',
      data   => '1',
      notify => Service['MpsSvc'],
    }

    registry::value { 'firewallpublic':
      key    => 'HKLM\SYSTEM\CurrentControlSet\Services\SharedAccess\Parameters\FirewallPolicy\PublicProfile',
      value  => 'EnableFirewall',
      type   => 'dword',
      data   => '1',
      notify => Service['MpsSvc'],
    }

# start Windows Firewall - Already defined in startservices so we will not define here
#    service { 'MpsSvc':
#      ensure => running,
#      enable => true,
#    }

    exec { 'disableRDP':
      command => 'netsh advfirewall firewall set rule name="Remote Desktop (TCP-In)" new enable=no',
      path    => 'C:\Windows\System32',
    }

    exec { 'disableSMB':
      command => 'netsh advfirewall firewall set rule name="File and Printer Sharing (SMB-In)" new enable=no',
      path    => 'C:\Windows\System32',
    }

  } else {
    notify {"This module runs only for Windows OS family. This host has OS family $::osfamily":}
  }
}
```

The successful test run is shown in the following screenshot:

```
C:\Users\puppet1>puppet agent --test
Info: Retrieving pluginfacts
Info: Retrieving plugin
Info: Loading facts
Info: Caching catalog for windowstest.example.local
Info: Applying configuration version '1432667152'
Notice: /Stage[main]/Winfirewall/Exec[disableSMB]/returns: executed successfully

Notice: /Stage[main]/Winfirewall/Exec[disableRDP]/returns: executed successfully

Notice: Finished catalog run in 3.84 seconds
```

In this section, we enabled the firewall profiles and their services. Further, we disabled some of the default rules for the services we do not want to use. Your needs may differ from this example, and you can add more rules here or remove some of the examples that we have defined.

Making the local administrator passwords unique

One of the problems of almost all companies is that the local admin passwords for Windows clients are the same for all clients. This implies that if you get one of the client computer's local admin password, you can use it for all the company computers. Further, if you are not using a disc encryption solution, obtaining the hash of the **Security Account Manager (SAM)** file password is very easy. The worse bit is that Windows enables the use of hash to authenticate, which means that you can directly use the hash to log in to other computers and do not need to crack the hash to get the real password. The solution to this problem is to differentiate the local admin password and make it unique for all your clients. This will ensure that one local admin password/hash is usable only for that computer.

In this section, we will create a `localadmin` module. The module will create a local user with admin rights for each computer. It will also generate a password that is unique to the computer. We will also create a function to generate the passwords.

The password function

The function name will be `hashpass`. As you will recall, we need to create our function under the `/etc/puppet/modules/stdlib/lib/puppet/parser/functions` folder.

The function details are shown in the following screenshot:

```
 1  # create a password unique to each computer
 2  module Puppet::Parser::Functions
 3    newfunction(:hashpass,:type => :rvalue, :doc => "Returns a SHA1.") do |args|
 4      require 'digest/sha1'
 5      value = 'justatext'
 6      value = value + lookupvar("fqdn")
 7      hash = Digest::SHA512.hexdigest(value)
 8      result = hash[4,10] + '.X'
 9      return result
10    end
11  end
```

We have already seen how to create a function in *Chapter 5, Puppet Facts, Functions, and Templates*, in the *Your first function* section. Thus, we will directly start with the hashing section, as follows:

- **Line 4**: As we are using the SHA algorithm, we need to include the relevant libraries.

- **Line 5 and 6**: We are using the **fully qualified domain name (FQDN)** of the computer and also including a text to make it unpredictable.

- **Line 7**: We are generating a hash from the string.

- **Line 8**: We are using the string of the hash beginning from the fifth character and including 10 characters after this. For example, the string is 1234567890abcdefgh. The result will be 567890abcd. We are also adding the extra character, '.X', to increase the complexity. Finally, the password becomes: 567890abcd.X.

- **Line 9**: This returns the value of the password.

The module

Now, we will write a simple module. This module will create a local user with administrator rights. For password generation, it will use our newly created function. The module structure is shown in the following screenshot:

```
root@puppetmaster:/etc/puppet/modules# tree localadmin/
localadmin/
└── manifests
    └── init.pp

1 directory, 1 file
root@puppetmaster:/etc/puppet/modules#
```

The module details are shown as follows:

```
# Create a local admin with unique password
class localadmin {
  $pass = hashpass()

  user { 'createlocaladmin':
    name     => 'lcladmin',
    password => $pass,
    groups   => 'Administrators',
  }
}
```

As we can see, this module is very simple. We are just calling the function to get our password and create a lcladmin user with that password.

The Ruby code to generate the password

"How to find the password?" is a question that would have popped up in your mind. We answer this by creating a small Ruby script, which is almost identical to our function. This code will get the FQDN and the extra text, justatext, we used as input and will generate the password. Under /etc/puppet/modules, we will create hash.rb as shown in the following screenshot:

```
1 require 'digest/sha1'
2
3 value2 = ARGV[0]
4 value3 = ARGV[2]
5 value = ARGV[1]
6 value = value + value2
7 hash = Digest::SHA512.hexdigest(value)
8 result = hash[4,10] + value3
9 puts result
```

As shown in the previous screenshot, this code is very similar to the hashpass function. However, we have made some changes. The first input argument is FQDN in line 3. The second argument is the justatext text that we used in the function. The last argument is the .x text that we have put at the end of the password. As we can see, even if somebody obtains this code, it will be very hard to generate the correct password. We did not put any documentation in this code on purpose.

The test

The following screenshot shows the results, when we run it on the host:

```
C:\Users\puppet1>puppet agent --test
Info: Retrieving pluginfacts
Info: Retrieving plugin
Notice: /File[C:/ProgramData/PuppetLabs/puppet/var/lib/puppet/parser/functions/.
hashpass.rb.swpl/ensure: removed
Info: Loading facts
Info: Caching catalog for windowstest.example.local
Info: Applying configuration version '1432672887'
Notice: /Stage[main]/Localadmin/User[Administrator]/password: created password
Notice: Finished catalog run in 0.12 seconds

C:\Users\puppet1>
```

Now, let's check the output of our `hash.rb` code in Puppet Master. In this example, the host that we run has the FQDN as `WINDOWSTEST.example.local`. Thus, the sample code to be executed is as follows:

```
$ rubyhash.rbWINDOWSTEST.example.localjustatext .X
```

To easily find the FQDN, you can use the following command:

```
C:\>facter fqdn
```

The resultant password is as obtained in the following screenshot:

```
root@puppetmaster:/etc/puppet/modules# ruby hash.rb WINDOWSTEST.example.local justatext .X
46737e758e.X
root@puppetmaster:/etc/puppet/modules#
```

Now, we can use the password obtained in the previous screenshot to log in to the host with the local admin.

Summary

In this chapter, we used many concepts together to put the hosts we manage in to an ideal state of security. The purpose was to prevent or hinder any hacking activity. We locked the startup folders for Windows users. We locked the hosts file. We also started the necessary services and stopped the unnecessary ones. Further, we tried to set our Windows Firewall to an ideal state. Finally, we made all the local administrator passwords unique.

In the next chapter, we will see reporting and monitoring of hosts.

7
Reporting and Monitoring

We dealt with many different scenarios and learned a lot of things in the first six chapters. We learned how to deal with users, services, and files. We learned how to write manifests, templates, and functions. We learned how to use these details for security. What we need to learn more about is how to check your hosts and their reports. Without any reporting, we cannot know the statuses of our hosts. We do not know whether our classes are implemented successfully or not, whether everything is as expected, or there are errors. Without these facts, we cannot say that everything is working as expected. In this chapter, we will learn how to check the following:

- The statuses of hosts from Foreman
- The report details of hosts from Foreman
- The statuses of hosts from the terminal
- The logs from the terminal

Checking the infrastructure statistics

In Foreman, we can check the general statistics of our infrastructure such as the OS distribution, architecture distribution, environment distribution, and number of CPUs. To display and access the statistics, select **Monitor** | **Statistics** from the top menu. A sample screenshot is provided as follows:

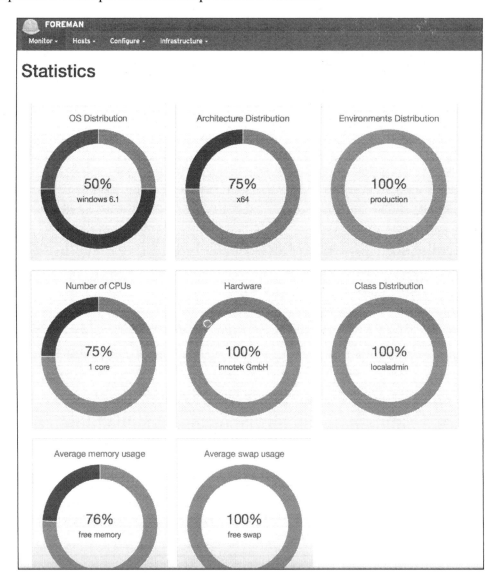

Checking the statuses of hosts from Foreman

We have already used Foreman interface many times in this book. We will now check its details for reporting purposes. The first thing we will check with Puppet is the general statuses of all the hosts. The general overview will show us a summary of all the hosts' statuses. We will see how many hosts have performed successful operations and how many of them failed. We can see the dashboard interface in Foreman from the **Monitor | Dashboard** top menu. The following is a screenshot of the dashboard:

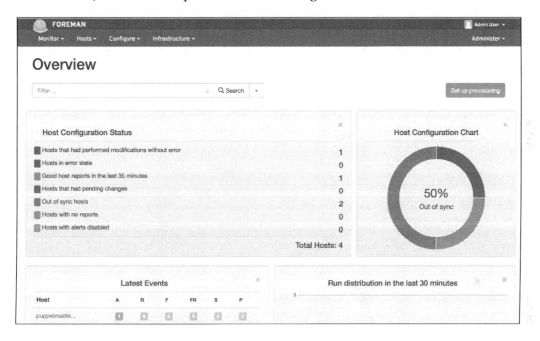

In this dashboard, we can see a general summary of all the hosts on the basis of following details:

- **Hosts that had performed modifications without error**: These are all the hosts that have modifications performed without any error in the last 35 minutes. Here is the search string for this:

  ```
  last_report > "35 minutes ago" and (status.applied > 0 or status.
  restarted > 0) and (status.failed = 0)
  ```

- **Hosts in error state**: Any host that has an error while implementing modifications in the last 35 minutes. Here is the search string for this:

  ```
  last_report > "35 minutes ago" and (status.failed > 0 or status.
  failed_restarts > 0) and status.enabled = true
  ```

- **Good host reports in the last 35 minutes**: These are the hosts that run the Puppet agent successfully without implementing any modifications. The search string is as follows:

```
last_report > "35 minutes ago" and status.enabled = true and
status.applied = 0 and status.failed = 0 and status.pending = 0
```

- **Hosts that had pending changes**: These are the hosts with pending status without any time limit. The search string is as follows:

```
status.pending > 0 and status.enabled = true
```

- **Out of sync hosts**: These are the hosts that did not connect to Puppet in the last 35 minutes. The search string is as follows:

```
last_report < "35 minutes ago" and status.enabled = true
```

- **Hosts with no reports**: These are the hosts without any report. These hosts may be newly added or they may also have a problem. The search string is as follows:

```
not has last_report and status.enabled = true
```

- **Hosts with alerts disabled**: These are the disabled hosts that display any alerts. The search string is as follows:

```
status.enabled = false
```

To see more details, you can click on one of the lines. For example, clicking on **Out of sync hosts** gives details similar to one shown in the following screenshot:

If one of the hosts in the previous screenshot shows that the servers are out of sync, it may imply a problem. In the case of the previous screenshot, these are client computers and it is possible that the user has shut them down.

In the next step, we can click on one of the hosts and see what happens with each click in more detail:

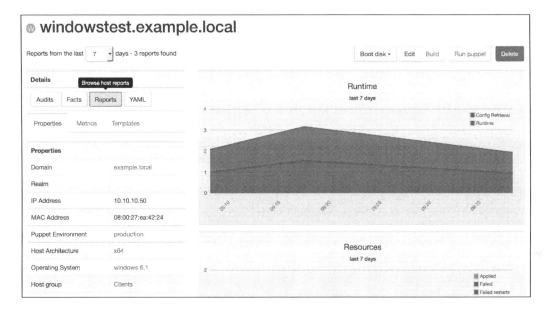

In general, we can see the **Runtime** and **Resources** graphics for the last seven days in the preceding screen. There are also tabs such as **Properties**, **Metrics**, and **Templates**. In the **Properties** tab, we can see some of the details of the host such as **Domain**, **IP Address**, **MAC address**, **Puppet Environment**, and **Operating System**. In the **Metrics** tab, we can see the number of the different report statuses:

Properties	Metrics	Templates

Report Status	
applied	1
restarted	0
failed	0
failed_restarts	0
skipped	0
pending	0

The **Templates** tab is related to provisioning and is out of scope. Lastly, we can see some buttons named **Audits**, **Fact Values**, **Reports**, and **YAML**. Let's check each of them.

Audits

In this section, we can see the administration activities handled for this host and when they were done. This information is important when you want to check the change details for a host. You can see who made the changes and its date details:

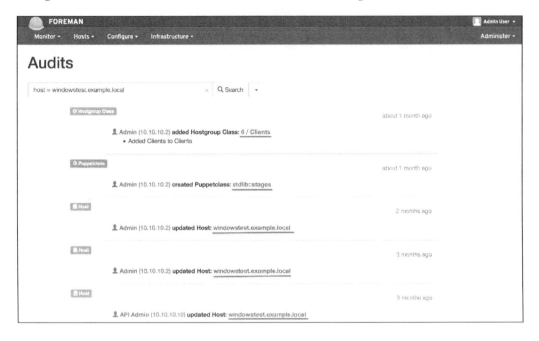

If you want to check one of the audits in more detail, you can click on them. In the previous screenshot, it is underlined where to click. After clicking the first line **6/Clients**, we can see more about the change details. In the following screenshot, we can see that for the **Clients** hostgroup, the **firewallon** class was assigned:

If you also want to see all the audit details that are not only related to the hosts, you can check this out from the **Monitor | Audits** top menu. Following is a screenshot for this. In general level audit, we can see information such as host, hostgroup, class additions, and deletions; you will also see new additions of operating systems and architecture. There are many more details in this audit list. I suggest that you review from the oldest to the newest. This will help you to understand what is going on in general:

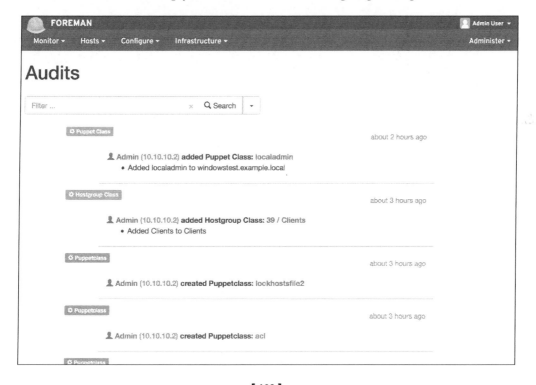

Facts

In this section, we can see all the fact details of a host. Here, the listed facts are the structured data about the relevant host. If you need to refresh your memory about facts, you can check the topic *Puppet facts* in *Chapter 5*, *Puppet Facts, Functions, and Templates*.

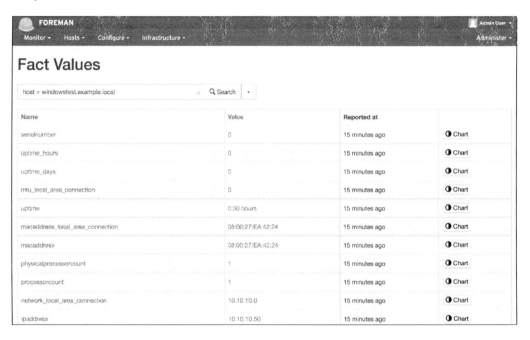

In the preceding screenshot, we can see the information such as the IP address, number of processors, MAC address, and uptime. You can get more useful information about the host such as the operating system, memory size, Puppet agent version, filesystems, your custom facts, partitions, FQDN, bios version, and virtualization info.

Reports

Here, we can see the reports list of the host. We will check out this part in more detail later in this chapter:

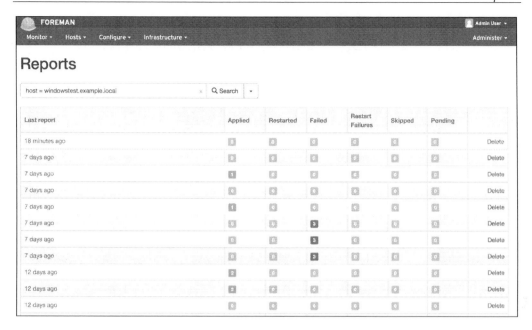

Last report	Applied	Restarted	Failed	Restart Failures	Skipped	Pending	
18 minutes ago	0	0	0	0	0	0	Delete
7 days ago	0	0	0	0	0	0	Delete
7 days ago	1	0	0	0	0	0	Delete
7 days ago	0	0	0	0	0	0	Delete
7 days ago	1	0	0	0	0	0	Delete
7 days ago	0	0	3	0	0	0	Delete
7 days ago	0	0	3	0	0	0	Delete
7 days ago	0	0	3	0	0	0	Delete
12 days ago	2	0	0	0	0	0	Delete
12 days ago	2	0	0	0	0	0	Delete
12 days ago	0	0	0	0	0	0	Delete

YAML

YAML is a recursive acronym for **YAML Ain't Markup Language**. YAML keeps the structured data of the host. In this, you can see which classes are assigned, the parameter values, and environment info:

```yaml
---
classes:
  helloworld:
  localadmin:
parameters:
  puppetmaster: puppetmaster.example.com
  hostgroup: Clients
  root_pw:
  foreman_env: production
  owner_name: Admin User
  owner_email: root@example.com
  foreman_subnets: []
  foreman_interfaces:
  - mac: 08:00:27:ea:42:24
    ip: 10.10.10.50
    type: Interface
    name:
    attrs: {}
    virtual: false
    link: true
    identifier:
    managed: true
    subnet:
environment: production
```

In this section, we saw how we can check the statuses of the hosts and get more information about them. In the next section, we will continue with the details of reporting.

Checking the report details of hosts from Foreman

Now, we will check more details about the reports. To check the reports, you can go to **Monitor** | **Reports** from the top menu. The default report list will display only the eventful reports. *Eventful* means that either of the following two events has occurred: a configuration change or an error.

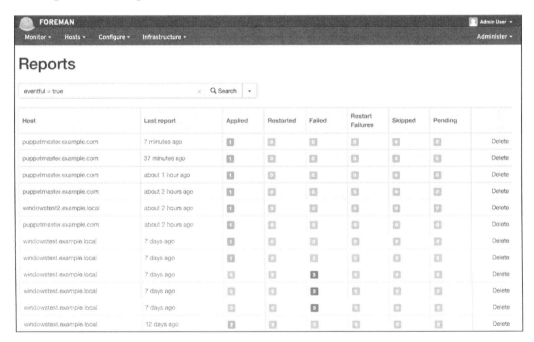

If there are no changes or errors, it will not be displayed in the default reports tab. To display all the reports, just remove `eventful = true` from the search, and run an empty search. You will have all the reports listed. You can see, in the following screenshot, the list of reports that have events or no events:

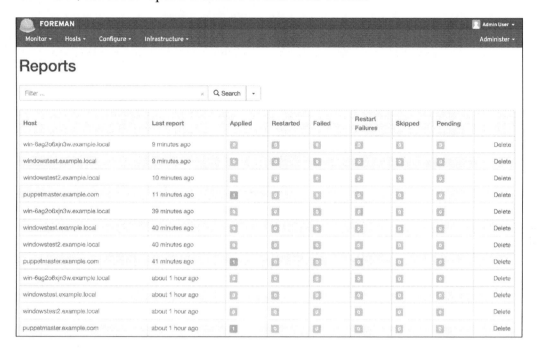

Now, let's check the details of a report with an error:

The first problem with the preceding report is that the server time and the client time are not same as seen in the highlighted area of the screenshot, **Host times seems to be adrift!**. To overcome this problem, I suggest that you install the ntp service on your Puppet Master server, so that it can accurately fetch the time and date details from Internet. The installation is very simple, just write this command in the terminal of Puppet Master:

```
$ sudo apt-get install ntp
```

You can also use the ntp module from Puppet Forge to install the ntp service. The details of the module can be found at https://forge.puppetlabs.com/ puppetlabs/ntp.

As we can see, the two errors in the list are about the password details of the user we are trying to create. This happened when we were trying to create a local administrator with a simple password. Here, Windows detected a failed criteria and did not let the user to be created. You may have also noticed that these details are also displayed when you run `puppet agent --test` in any host that the class is assigned to. In the reports, you can find the older runs and see what happened.

The following is another report with a successful `apply` event .Let's check the details of this report:

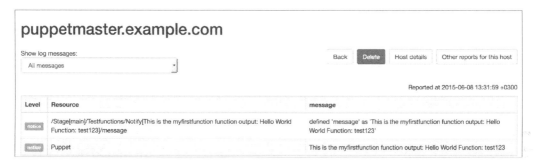

In this report, we can see that the apply events have only level notice; and the event only displays a notify message. Also, it is possible to have reports without any events. The following is a screenshot of an uneventful report:

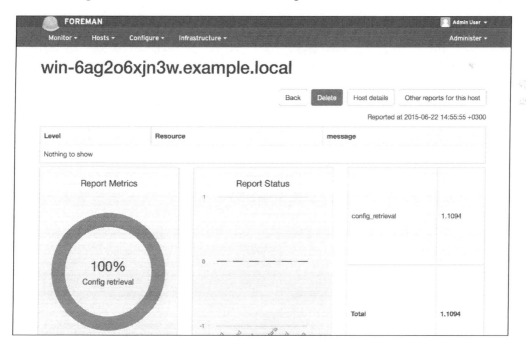

As we can see, this is giving a **Nothing to show** message. We completed the different aspects of reports in Foreman and learned how to check the report details. As you can see, it is very easy with Foreman to check the reports and their details.

Checking the statuses of hosts from the terminal

We checked the features of the Foreman interface. Now, it is time to check the details from the terminal. You may not need these details, as Foreman is enough for your daily management. However, sometimes Foreman may not be enough and you may need to troubleshoot. In this section, we will see the details of hosts as they are recognized correctly by Puppet via node.rb. In this, there are the node definitions, facts files for hosts, and signed certificates.

node.rb

node.rb under /etc/puppet/node.rb is one of the tools that we can use to check whether the related host is accurately defined and has no problems. node.rb is Foreman-specific and will only work with it. You need to run it with root rights. The command usage is as follows:

```
$ sudo -i
# /etc/puppet/node.rb hostname
```

If the preceding command gives error in your environment, because Ruby was not added at the beginning, the following command will work:

```
# ruby /etc/puppet/node.rb hostname
```

The following screenshot shows the result of `node.rb`:

```
root@puppetmaster:/etc/puppet# exit
logout
puppet@puppetmaster:~$ /etc/puppet/node.rb puppetmaster.example.com
---
classes:
  testfunctions:
parameters:
  puppetmaster: puppetmaster.example.com
  hostgroup: Servers/Linux Servers
  root_pw:
  foreman_env: production
  owner_name: Admin User
  owner_email: root@example.com
  foreman_subnets: []
  foreman_interfaces:
- mac: 08:00:27:67:57:d4
  ip: 10.10.10.10
  type: Interface
  name:
  attrs: {}
  virtual: false
  link: true
  identifier: eth0
  managed: true
  subnet:
environment: production
puppet@puppetmaster:~$ 
```

The host YAML files

These files have the host config details in a YAML file. The folder for them is `/var/lib/puppet/yaml/foreman`. The following screenshot shows the folder details:

```
root@puppetmaster:/var/lib/puppet/yaml/foreman# ls -l
total 32
-rw-r--r-- 1 puppet puppet 119 Jun  8 18:02 puppetmaster.example.com-push-facts.yaml
-rw-r--r-- 1 puppet puppet 460 Jun  8 18:13 puppetmaster.example.com.yaml
-rw-r--r-- 1 puppet puppet 119 Jun  8 13:33 win-6ag2o6xjn3w.example.local-push-facts.yaml
-rw-r--r-- 1 puppet puppet 386 Jun  8 13:33 win-6ag2o6xjn3w.example.local.yaml
-rw-r--r-- 1 puppet puppet 119 Jun  8 13:33 windowstest2.example.local-push-facts.yaml
-rw-r--r-- 1 puppet puppet 382 Jun  8 18:01 windowstest2.example.local.yaml
-rw-r--r-- 1 puppet puppet 119 Jun  8 13:33 windowstest.example.local-push-facts.yaml
-rw-r--r-- 1 puppet puppet 454 Jun  8 13:33 windowstest.example.local.yaml
root@puppetmaster:/var/lib/puppet/yaml/foreman# 
```

Now, let's check one of the YAML file for a host. We will use "less filename" to display the contents of a file. In our example, we can again check `puppetmaster.example.com`. The command is as follows:

```
# less puppetmaster.example.com.yaml
```

The contents of the file are as shown in the following screenshot. You can also check the details with the `node.rb` output, and can see that they have identical results:

```
---
classes:
  testfunctions:
parameters:
  puppetmaster: puppetmaster.example.com
  hostgroup: Servers/Linux Servers
  root_pw:
  foreman_env: production
  owner_name: Admin User
  owner_email: root@example.com
  foreman_subnets: []
  foreman_interfaces:
  - mac: 08:00:27:67:57:d4
    ip: 10.10.10.10
    type: Interface
    name:
    attrs: {}
    virtual: false
    link: true
    identifier: eth0
    managed: true
    subnet:
environment: production
puppetmaster.example.com.yaml (END)
```

There is also another file for every host ending with `-push-facts.yaml`. This file shows the time when the details are pushed. Here are the details of `puppetmaster.example.com-push-facts.yaml`:

```
Facts from this host were last pushed to https://puppetmaster.example.com/api/hosts/facts at 2015-06-08 18:02:03 +0300
puppetmaster.example.com-push-facts.yaml (END)
```

Facts

A copy of facts submitted to the master from the agents, when requesting a catalog, is available in the `var/lib/puppet/yaml/facts` folder. You can check their details again with the `less` command:

```
# less puppetmaster.example.com.yaml
```

```
--- !ruby/object:Puppet::Node::Facts
 name: puppetmaster.example.com
 values:
   lsbdistdescription: "Ubuntu 14.04.2 LTS"
   id: root
   hardwareisa: x86_64
   kernel: Linux
   interfaces: "eth0,lo"
   ipaddress_eth0: "10.10.10.10"
   macaddress_eth0: "08:00:27:67:57:d4"
   netmask_eth0: "255.255.255.0"
   mtu_eth0: "1500"
   ipaddress_lo: "127.0.0.1"
   netmask_lo: "255.0.0.0"
   mtu_lo: "65536"
   system_uptime: "{\x22seconds\x22=>28811, \x22hours\x22=>8, \x22days\x22=>0, \x22uptime\x22=>\x228:00 hours\x22}"
   blockdevice_sda_size: "42949672960"
   blockdevice_sda_vendor: ATA
   blockdevice_sda_model: "VBOX HARDDISK"
   blockdevice_sr0_size: "58241024"
   blockdevice_sr0_vendor: VBOX
   blockdevice_sr0_model: CD-ROM
   blockdevices: "sda,sr0"
   network_eth0: "10.10.10.0"
   network_lo: "127.0.0.0"
   kernelmajversion: "3.16"
   rubyplatform: x86_64-linux
   filesystems: "ext2,ext3,ext4,vfat"
   uptime_days: "0"
   operatingsystem: Ubuntu
   lsbdistrelease: "14.04"
   lsbdistid: Ubuntu
   hostname: puppetmaster
   processors: "{\x22models\x22=>[\x22Intel(R) Core(TM) i7-3740QM CPU @ 2.70GHz\x22, \x22Intel(R) Core(TM) i7-3740QM CPU @
2.70GHz\x22], \x22count\x22=>2, \x22physicalcount\x22=>1}"
   architecture: amd64
   hardwaremodel: x86_64
puppetmaster.example.com.yaml
```

The Puppet SSL certificates

The SSL certificate details for Puppet are in the `/var/lib/puppet/ssl/` folder:

```
root@puppetmaster:/var/lib/puppet/ssl# ls -l
total 28
drwxr-xr-x 5 puppet puppet 4096 Feb 23 18:23 ca
drwxr-xr-x 2 puppet puppet 4096 Feb 23 18:23 certificate_requests
drwxr-xr-x 2 puppet puppet 4096 Apr 13 19:47 certs
-rw-r--r-- 1 puppet puppet 1210 Apr 13 19:47 crl.pem
drwxr-x--- 2 puppet puppet 4096 Feb 23 18:23 private
drwxr-x--- 2 puppet puppet 4096 Feb 23 18:23 private_keys
drwxr-xr-x 2 puppet puppet 4096 Feb 23 18:23 public_keys
root@puppetmaster:/var/lib/puppet/ssl#
```

The signed certificates of the hosts are under the `/var/lib/puppet/ssl/ca/signed` folder:

```
root@puppetmaster:/var/lib/puppet/ssl/ca/signed# ls -l
total 16
-rw-r--r-- 1 puppet puppet 2065 Feb 23 18:23 puppetmaster.example.com.pem
-rw-r--r-- 1 puppet puppet 1984 Mar 17 19:25 win-6ag2o6xjn3w.example.local.pem
-rw-r--r-- 1 puppet puppet 1980 Mar 17 19:25 windowstest2.example.local.pem
-rw-r--r-- 1 puppet puppet 1980 Apr 21 14:54 windowstest.example.local.pem
root@puppetmaster:/var/lib/puppet/ssl/ca/signed#
```

These certificates become important when you have problems with them. For example, sometimes the certificate in the host and in Puppet Master does not match. In this case, you check the details here.

Checking the logs from the terminal

There are not many details to discover in the terminal for reporting. However, there are logs that are not displayed in Foreman. We may need to check these logs for troubleshooting purpose. The logs that we will check are under the var/log/ apache2 folder. The following screenshot shows the contents of this folder:

```
root@puppetmaster:/var/log/apache2# ls -l
total 1704
-rw-r----- 1 root adm        0 Feb 23 19:30 access.log
-rw-r--r-- 1 root root       0 Feb 23 19:43 default_error.log
-rw-r----- 1 root adm   178961 Jun  8 18:01 error.log
-rw-r--r-- 1 root root    5475 Jun  8 11:32 foreman_access.log
-rw-r--r-- 1 root root       0 Feb 23 19:43 foreman_error.log
-rw-r--r-- 1 root root  802671 Jun  8 19:57 foreman-ssl_access_ssl.log
-rw-r--r-- 1 root root       0 Feb 23 19:43 foreman-ssl_error_ssl.log
-rw-r----- 1 root adm        0 Feb 23 19:30 other_vhosts_access.log
-rw-r--r-- 1 root root  723318 Jun  8 19:57 puppet_access_ssl.log
-rw-r--r-- 1 root root   14980 Jun  8 11:32 puppet_error_ssl.log
root@puppetmaster:/var/log/apache2#
```

As we can see from the preceding screenshot, there are some logs with zero byte size. We do not need to check these files. When we check the apache config, we will see that there are different sites enabled under /etc/apache2/sites-enabled/:

```
root@puppetmaster:/var/log/apache2# ls -l /etc/apache2/sites-enabled/
total 0
lrwxrwxrwx 1 root root 44 Feb 23 19:42 05-foreman.conf -> /etc/apache2/sites-available/05-foreman.conf
lrwxrwxrwx 1 root root 48 Feb 23 19:42 05-foreman-ssl.conf -> /etc/apache2/sites-available/05-foreman-ssl.conf
lrwxrwxrwx 1 root root 44 Feb 23 19:42 15-default.conf -> /etc/apache2/sites-available/15-default.conf
lrwxrwxrwx 1 root root 43 Feb 23 19:42 25-puppet.conf -> /etc/apache2/sites-available/25-puppet.conf
root@puppetmaster:/var/log/apache2#
```

You can match the config files with the log files, as follows:

- 05-foreman.conf file is for the port 80 access and it is logged under the foreman_access.log and foreman_error.log files.

- 05-foreman-ssl.conf file is for the port 443 access and it is logged under the foreman-ssl_access.log and foreman-ssl_error.log files.

- 25-puppet.conf file is for the port 8140 access and it is logged under the 25-puppet_access_ssl.log and puppet_error_ssl.log files.

- 15-default.conf is the default config file. This one is not used for Puppet or Foreman.

You can also check out each config file and see that the logging config was set in it. The following screenshot shows an example for the `25-puppet.conf` file details:

```
# ***************************************
# Vhost template in module puppetlabs-apache
# Managed by Puppet
# ***************************************

<VirtualHost *:8140>
  ServerName puppet

  ## Vhost docroot
  DocumentRoot "/etc/puppet/rack/public/"


  ## Directories, there should at least be a declaration for /etc/puppet/rack/public/


  <Directory "/etc/puppet/rack/public/">
    AllowOverride None
    Require all granted
    PassengerEnabled On
  </Directory>

  ## Load additional static includes


  ## Logging
  ErrorLog "/var/log/apache2/puppet_error_ssl.log"
  ServerSignature Off
  CustomLog "/var/log/apache2/puppet_access_ssl.log" combined
```

When you want to see what happens in one of the logs in real time, it is a good idea to use the `tail` command. With the `-f` flag, it will display the last 10 lines, and whenever there are new records, it will display them in real time. The following screenshot shows an example screen:

```
root@puppetmaster:/var/log/apache2# tail -f puppet_access_ssl.log
10.10.10.10 - - [08/Jun/2015:19:57:16 +0300] "GET /production/node/puppetmaster.example.com?transaction_uuid=ae3348e4-c3a9-4fd9-8ab6-77bf16d1172
2&fail_on_404=true HTTP/1.1" 200 5634 "-" "Ruby"
10.10.10.10 - - [08/Jun/2015:19:57:16 +0300] "GET /production/file_metadatas/pluginfacts?links=manage&recurse=true&ignore=.svn&ignore=CVS&ignore
=.git&checksum_type=md5 HTTP/1.1" 200 302 "-" "Ruby"
10.10.10.10 - - [08/Jun/2015:19:57:17 +0300] "GET /production/file_metadatas/plugins?links=manage&recurse=true&ignore=.svn&ignore=CVS&ignore=.gi
t&checksum_type=md5 HTTP/1.1" 200 48899 "-" "Ruby"
10.10.10.10 - - [08/Jun/2015:19:57:18 +0300] "POST /production/catalog/puppetmaster.example.com HTTP/1.1" 200 1150 "-" "Ruby"
10.10.10.10 - - [08/Jun/2015:19:57:19 +0300] "PUT /production/report/puppetmaster.example.com HTTP/1.1" 200 11 "-" "Ruby"
10.10.10.10 - - [08/Jun/2015:20:27:16 +0300] "GET /production/node/puppetmaster.example.com?transaction_uuid=d72f2b88-932a-4be7-b090-3e27b5c82f1
e&fail_on_404=true HTTP/1.1" 200 5686 "-" "Ruby"
10.10.10.10 - - [08/Jun/2015:20:27:17 +0300] "GET /production/file_metadatas/pluginfacts?links=manage&recurse=true&ignore=.svn&ignore=CVS&ignore
=.git&checksum_type=md5 HTTP/1.1" 200 302 "-" "Ruby"
10.10.10.10 - - [08/Jun/2015:20:27:17 +0300] "GET /production/file_metadatas/plugins?links=manage&recurse=true&ignore=.svn&ignore=CVS&ignore=.gi
t&checksum_type=md5 HTTP/1.1" 200 48899 "-" "Ruby"
10.10.10.10 - - [08/Jun/2015:20:27:19 +0300] "POST /production/catalog/puppetmaster.example.com HTTP/1.1" 200 1150 "-" "Ruby"
10.10.10.10 - - [08/Jun/2015:20:27:20 +0300] "PUT /production/report/puppetmaster.example.com HTTP/1.1" 200 11 "-" "Ruby"
```

If you want to see the error logs, you can also check out the contents of the logs that contain `error` in the name.

To see all the Apache logs details for a specific host, you can use the following command:

```
# cat * | grep -r puppetmaster.example.com | less
```

You can also replace the `puppetmaster.example.com` hostname with any specific term that you search for.

Summary

In this chapter, we learned how to see the statuses of hosts in the summary, and after this, we checked the information available for the hosts. We also checked the reporting details of Foreman. After this, we switched to the terminal and checked the definitions, statuses, and facts of the hosts. Finally, we checked the access and error logs for Foreman and Puppet that are generated by Apache.

In the next chapter, we will see how we can automatically install and update software using Chocolatey with Puppet.

8
Installing Software and Updates

In this last chapter, we will learn how to install, update, and uninstall a software. We will also automate these processes as much as possible. You will learn the following topics:

- How to install a software with Puppet
- What is Chocolatey
- How to install and update a software with Chocolatey
- How to use Chocolatey and Puppet together to install/update the mostly used softwares
- How to update Puppet agents
- How to uninstall a software using Chocolatey

Installing a software with package resource

We will begin by understanding how to install a software with Puppet. Here, the idea is to create one class to install the application on all the hosts, so that you do not need to repeat the task on hundreds of computers.

However, we will need some preparations first. We will need to install the software on a sample host and remember the name of the installation. The installation name will be used as the package name. We will use a simple software called **Workrave** as an example. This tiny software helps users to have micro rests and prevent "repetitive stress injury". You can download the software from `http://www.workrave.org/download/`.

We need to download the Windows installer:

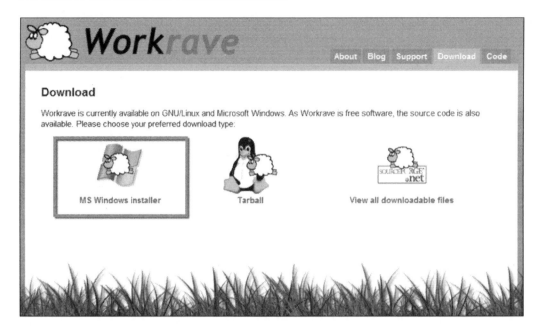

After downloading the installer, we will install it on one of our test hosts. This will provide us with the installation details that we need for our Puppet module:

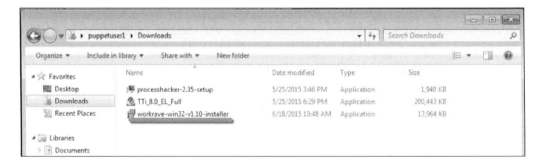

Double-click the installation file and install it by selecting the **Next**, **Accept**, and **OK** buttons, whichever you see. After installing it on the test host, we will need to learn how to install it silently. The silent installation is needed so that when we push the software to the hosts, the users are not disturbed by the installation screens that are awaiting input. To find the software, first, we try to find out the help details from the command line:

```
"C:\Users\puppet1\Downloads>workrave-win32-v1.10-installer.exe /?"
```

This will be unsuccessful for this installer. Normally, for numerous installers, this step gives the options that show how to install it silently. If you do not find any details, the next option is to search the Internet. When we search for `workrave unattended install`, we can find out that it is using Inno Setup. The following link shows the details for the Inno Setup switches: `http://unattended.sourceforge.net/InnoSetup_Switches_ExitCodes.html`. Checking out the documentation reveals that the `'/VERYSILENT'` switch can be used. Using this information, we can try to silently install the software from the command line:

```
C:\Users\puppet1\Downloads>workrave-win32-v1.10-installer.exe /verysilent
```

Now, it is time to learn how Puppet sees this new installation. Thus, we will use the following command. This command will list all the installed software:

```
C:\>puppet resource package
```

The output can be seen in the following screenshot:

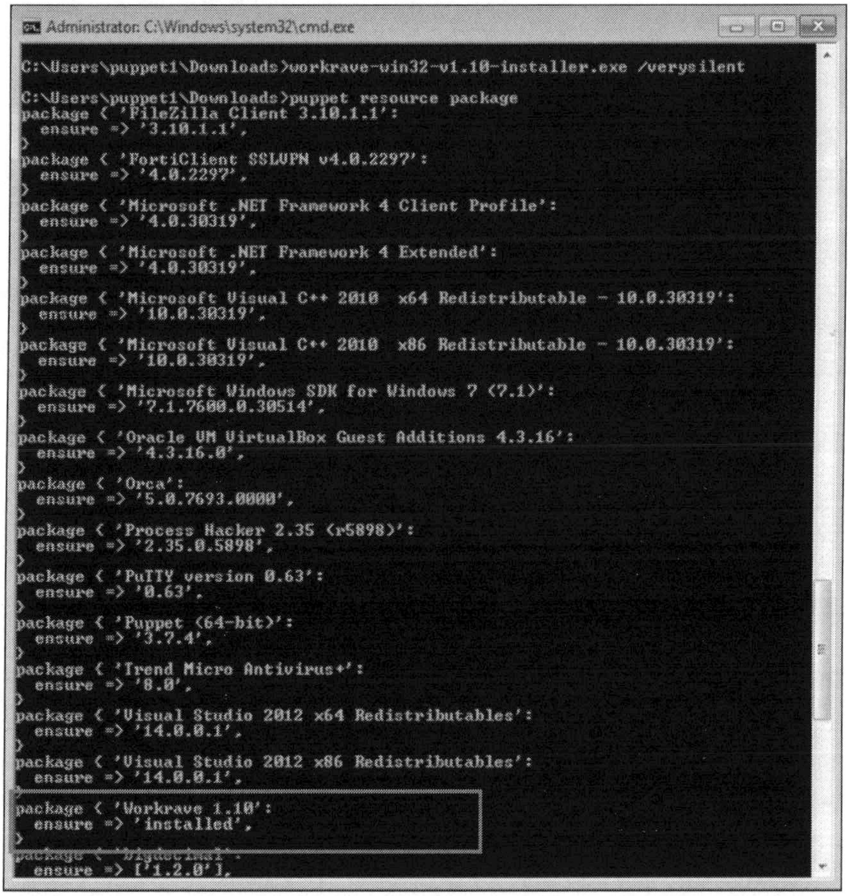

As you can see, Workrave details are also present. These are the details that we will use in our module. If you do not want to use the command to get these details, you can also check out **Control Panel** for a list of all the softwares. We can see in the next screenshot that the names of the installed software match with the command output. The advantage of using the command output is that you can just copy and paste the code here:

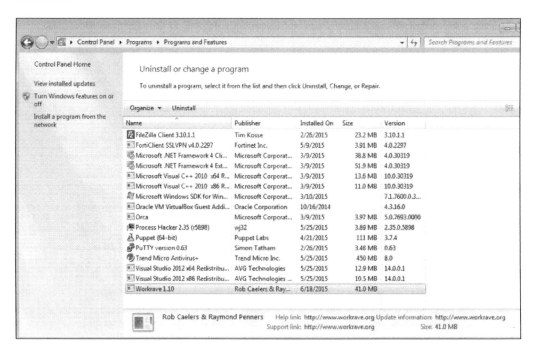

Now, we can continue with writing our module as we have collected enough information. The package resource type in Puppet can install or uninstall a software. Here is the sample code:

```
package { 'Software name as we see in installation details':
  ensure          => installed,
  source          => 'installation file path and name',
  install_options => ['installparamater1','installparamater2'],
}
```

After learning the basic structure, let's create our module. We will use installworkrave as the module name. We will also create the files folder in this and put our installation file here. Here is the structure:

```
root@puppetmaster:/etc/puppet/modules# tree installworkrave/
installworkrave/
├── files
│   └── workrave-win32-v1.10-installer.exe
└── manifests
    └── init.pp

2 directories, 2 files
root@puppetmaster:/etc/puppet/modules#
```

Here are the manifest details:

```
# install workrave
class installworkrave {
  file { 'c:/windows/temp/workrave-win32-v1.10-installer.exe':
    source            => 'puppet:///modules/installworkrave/workrave-win32-v1.10-installer.exe',
    source_permissions => ignore,
  }
  package { 'Workrave 1.10':
    ensure          => installed,
    source          => 'c:/windows/temp/workrave-win32-v1.10-installer.exe',
    install_options => ['/VERYSILENT'],
    require         => File['c:/windows/temp/workrave-win32-v1.10-installer.exe'],
  }
}
```

As you can see in the previous screenshot, we also included a `file` upload section. We need the installation file on the host, otherwise, Puppet cannot install it. So, we first upload the file to the host's `C:\Windows\Temp` directory and then, we show it as the source file for the installation. We also use `/VERYSILENT` as the installation option, so that the installation takes place in the background.

Now, it is time for a test run. As you can see, it successfully uploads the installation file and installs the software:

```
C:\Users\puppet1\Downloads>puppet agent --test
Info: Retrieving pluginfacts
Info: Retrieving plugin
Info: Loading facts
Info: Caching catalog for windowstest.example.local
Info: Applying configuration version '1433804341'
Notice: /Stage[main]/Installworkrave/File[c:/windows/temp/workrave-win32-v1.10-i
nstaller.exe]/ensure: defined content as '{md5}224bf275ddcd5c9603da28d74e8f336d'

Notice: /Stage[main]/Installworkrave/Package[Workrave 1.10]/ensure: created
Notice: Finished catalog run in 6.67 seconds

C:\Users\puppet1\Downloads>
```

We completed installing the software using the `Package` type. Next, we will continue with easier ways of installation using Chocolatey.

What is Chocolatey?

Chocolatey is a package manager for Windows. There are commands for Linux such as `apt-get` and `yum` for package management. They are very easy to use. Whenever you need to install something, you just write `apt-get install packagename` or `yum install packagename`. Here, the idea is to have a similar functionality in Windows. You can see more details about Chocolatey at `https://chocolatey.org`.

After learning what Chocolatey is, we will install it manually and install some software using this. In the later sections, we will see how to use Chocolatey with Puppet.

Installing Chocolatey

The installation of Chocolatey is very simple. You can see the following details on the previous link:

Open Command Prompt with administrator rights and copy and paste the following command:

```
C:\> @powershell -NoProfile -ExecutionPolicy Bypass -Command "iex ((new-
object net.webclient).DownloadString('https://chocolatey.org/install.
ps1'))" && SET PATH=%PATH%;%ALLUSERSPROFILE%\chocolatey\bin
```

The output of this installation command is shown in the following screenshot. As you can see, the installation is very easy. After installing Chocolatey, just close Command Prompt and open a new one:

Now, write the following command to see if Chocolatey is installed and it is giving the output:

```
C:\> choco --version
```

The following screenshot verifies its functionality:

```
C:\Users\puppet1>choco --version
0.9.9.8

C:\Users\puppet1>_
```

Installing a software with Chocolatey

Now, let's try to install a software with Chocolatey. To do this, we need to know the package name. For example, assume that we want to install Notepad++. Let's check this out at `https://chocolatey.org/`. Searching for `notepad` brings the details as shown in the following screenshot:

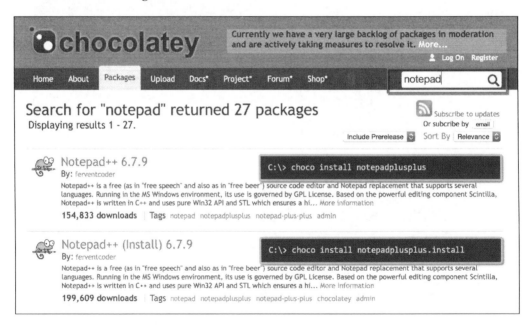

As you can see, there are two results for the same version. The package ending with **.install** is for portable installations. We will use the regular one. We can see how to install Notepad++ in the following screenshot. The command is as follows:

```
C:\> choco install notepadplusplus
```

In the following screenshot, we can see the installation steps and output:

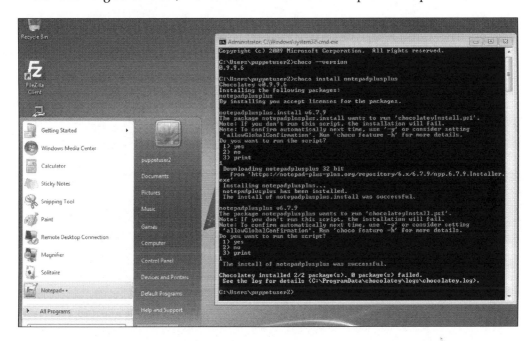

Uninstalling a software with Chocolatey

Chocolatey, also, has the option to uninstall the installed packages. However, there are some exceptions such as:

- The software to be uninstalled must be installed using Chocolatey
- The software choco package must have its uninstall script

As you can see, the uninstall part may not work properly. Let's check the details for Notepad++. On the Web, check the details for the package. In the **Files** section, there must be an uninstall script, otherwise, the uninstall will not work correctly. It means that when you want to uninstall it, you need to do it manually:

Now, let's check out another software that we can install and uninstall. This time we will check out 7-Zip. Here are the details of 7-Zip:

As you can see in the previous screenshot, this has the uninstall file. Now, let's try to install and uninstall. The following is the installation screenshot:

```
C:\Users\puppetuser2>choco install 7zip.install -y
Chocolatey v0.9.9.6
Installing the following packages:
7zip.install
By installing you accept licenses for the packages.

7zip.install v9.38
 WARNING: This installer is known to close the explorer process. This means
 you may lose current work.
 If it doesn't automatically restart explorer, type 'explorer' on the
 command shell to restart it.
 Installing 7zip.install...
 7zip.install has been installed.
 The install of 7zip.install was successful.

Chocolatey installed 1/1 package(s). 0 package(s) failed.
 See the log for details (C:\ProgramData\chocolatey\logs\chocolatey.log).

C:\Users\puppetuser2>
```

As you can see in the following screenshot, it seems to have been uninstalled successfully:

```
C:\Users\puppetuser2>choco uninstall 7zip.install -y
Chocolatey v0.9.9.6
Uninstalling the following packages:
7zip.install

7zip.install v9.38
 Uninstalling (23170F69-40C1-2702-0938-000001000000)...
 (23170F69-40C1-2702-0938-000001000000) has been uninstalled.
 Skipping auto uninstaller - AutoUninstaller feature is not enabled.
 7zip.install has been successfully uninstalled.

Chocolatey uninstalled 1/1 packages. 0 packages failed.
 See the log for details (C:\ProgramData\chocolatey\logs\chocolatey.log).

C:\Users\puppetuser2>
```

Normally, all the packages should also have an uninstall package. However, never assume this and check whether it can be uninstalled correctly. When checked, you will see that most of the packages do not have an uninstall option. So the uninstall functionality of Chocolatey is not dependable at the moment. Another important point is that choco uninstall will not give errors, even if it does not uninstall the package.

Using Chocolatey to install a software

After learning Chocolatey and its limits, we will continue with using Chocolatey with Puppet. Using both of them together will be a great plus for us and all the installation process will be much easier. When we manage installations with Chocolatey in Puppet, we will not need to find the installation package, its version, and how to run it silently. The installation will be completed with a very little effort.

To use Chocolatey with Puppet, there is a module from Puppet Forge that we need to install. Go to Puppet Forge website and search for `Chocolatey`. You can see the module in the following screenshot. We will install the `chocolatey/chocolatey` module:

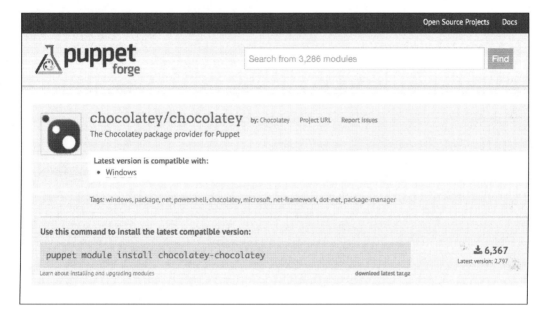

To install the module, go to Puppet Master, open a terminal window, and run the following command:

```
# sudo puppet module install chocolatey-chocolatey
```

The following screenshot shows a successful installation:

```
puppet@puppetmaster:~$ sudo puppet module install chocolatey-chocolatey
[sudo] password for puppet:
Notice: Preparing to install into /etc/puppet/modules ...
Notice: Downloading from https://forgeapi.puppetlabs.com ...
Notice: Installing -- do not interrupt ...
/etc/puppet/modules
└── chocolatey-chocolatey (v1.0.0)
puppet@puppetmaster:~$ ▊
```

Now, it is time to install a software using Chocolatey. For this purpose, we need to write a module. A sample manifest is as follows:

```
package { 'notepadplusplus':
  ensure            => installed|latest|'1.0.0'|absent,
  provider          => 'chocolatey',
  install_options   => ['-pre','-params','"','param1','param2','"'],
  uninstall_options => ['-r'],
  source            => 'https://myfeed.example.com/api/v2',
}
```

Now, let's check the details step by step:

- `package { 'notepadplusplus':` Here, we define the package name that is listed in `https://chocolatey.org/`.

- `ensure`: Here, you have different options. `installed` makes sure that it is installed. `latest` updates the software whenever there is a new version at `https://chocolatey.org/`. If you give the version number, such as `'1.0.0'`, it will install this version. `absent` uninstalls the package. Do not trust the uninstall functionality as we have mentioned previously!

- `provider => 'chocolatey'`: Here, we change the package provider so that the installation is handled by Chocolatey.

- `install_options`: Normally, the Chocolatey packages are installed silently. However, you also have the option to use different installation options.

- `uninstall_options`: Here you can put different options, for the uninstallation.

- `source`: We will not use this one. However, if you have different sources or your own Chocolatey server, you can reference it here.

The following is a more simple form that we will normally use. As you can see, it is very simple to install software using Chocolatey:

```
package { 'notepadplusplus':
  ensure   => installed,
  provider => 'chocolatey',
}
```

As you will remember, we used Workrave as an example before. Now, let's write a new module that uses Chocolatey, and then compare it with our default first module to see the differences. We will create a new module named chocoworkrave. The module structure is as shown in the following screenshot:

```
root@puppetmaster:/etc/puppet/modules# tree chocoworkrave/
chocoworkrave/
└── manifests
    └── init.pp

1 directory, 1 file
root@puppetmaster:/etc/puppet/modules# 
```

Our old module structure, installworkrave, is shown in the following screenshot:

```
root@puppetmaster:/etc/puppet/modules# tree installworkrave/
installworkrave/
├── files
│   └── workrave-win32-v1.10-installer.exe
└── manifests
    └── init.pp

2 directories, 2 files
root@puppetmaster:/etc/puppet/modules# 
```

Here, we can already see that there is less effort required. We do not need to find and upload the installation file. The following screenshot shows the manifest details for chocoworkrave:

```
# install workrave with chocolatey
class chocoworkrave {
  package { 'workrave':
    ensure   => installed,
    provider => 'chocolatey',
  }
}
```

The following manifest shows the details for `installworkrave`:

```
# install workrave
class installworkrave {
  file { 'c:/windows/temp/workrave-win32-v1.10-installer.exe':
    source            => 'puppet:///modules/installworkrave/workrave-win32-v1.10-installer.exe',
    source_permissions => ignore,
  }
  package { 'Workrave 1.10':
    ensure            => installed,
    source            => 'c:/windows/temp/workrave-win32-v1.10-installer.exe',
    install_options   => ['/VERYSILENT'],
    require           => File['c:/windows/temp/workrave-win32-v1.10-installer.exe'],
  }
}
```

As you can see, more effort is required with the default provider. You need to find the exact name of the installation. You need to download the installation and upload it to server. You need to send the installation to the host. You need to give the installation options. When you have `Chocolatey` as provider, you just need to know the package name.

> The `workrave` package for Chocolatey has problems, and is not working properly. So, if you see that your installation is not working properly, do not spend time with it.

Installing Firefox as an example

First, search Chocolatey for Firefox and find the relevant package:

In our example, as you can see in the previous screenshot, the name of the package is firefox. Now, let's write our module. We can use chocofirefox as a name for our module. The structure of the module is shown in the following screenshot:

```
root@puppetmaster:/etc/puppet/modules# tree chocofirefox/
chocofirefox/
└── manifests
    └── init.pp

1 directory, 1 file
root@puppetmaster:/etc/puppet/modules# 
```

The manifest details are shown in the following screenshot:

```
# install firefox using chocolatey
class chocofirefox {
  package { 'firefox':
    ensure   => installed,
    provider => 'chocolatey',
  }
}
```

Further, the test results are shown in the following screenshot. We can see that the installation was a success:

```
Administrator: C:\Windows\system32\cmd.exe
Microsoft Windows [Version 6.1.7600]
Copyright (c) 2009 Microsoft Corporation.  All rights reserved.

C:\Users\puppet1>puppet agent --test
Info: Retrieving pluginfacts
Info: Retrieving plugin
Info: Loading facts
Info: Caching catalog for windowstest.example.local
Info: Applying configuration version '1433808905'
Notice: /Stage[main]/Chocofirefox/Package[firefox]/ensure: created
Notice: Finished catalog run in 48.18 seconds

C:\Users\puppet1>
```

Installing Chocolatey using Puppet

It may occur to you that installation of Chocolatey to each host may be a burden. To install Chocolatey automatically on each host, you can use a module named ceritsc/chocolatey_sw in Puppet Forge. After the installation of this module, if you assign this module to any of your hosts or host groups, Chocolatey will be installed on them.

Using Chocolatey to update a software

One of the challenges for IT is to keep the client software up to date. It is easy for Windows updates that can be handled automatically. However, when it comes to third-party softwares, the updates may become a burden. Next, we will see how Puppet and Chocolatey deal with updates.

As an example, we will use the Java Runtime installation. We will first install an older version and see whether it is updated correctly. Here is the package that we will use:

When we scroll down, we will also see some older versions. We will first install the older version, 7.0.75. We will do it manually from Command Prompt:

Tags

java runtime environment

Version History

Version	Downloads	Last updated	Status
Java Runtime (JRE) 8.0.40	37344	**Tuesday, March 24, 2015**	approved
Java Runtime (JRE) 7.0.75	36946	**Tuesday, January 20, 2015**	approved
Java Runtime (JRE) 7.0.71	33383	**Wednesday, October 15, 2014**	approved
Java Runtime (JRE) 7.0.67.20140930	10899	**Tuesday, September 30, 2014**	
Java Runtime (JRE) 7.0.67.20140907	11577	**Saturday, September 6, 2014**	
Java Runtime (JRE) 7.0.67	11504	**Tuesday, August 5, 2014**	
Java Runtime (JRE) 7.0.65.20140715	6277	**Tuesday, July 15, 2014**	
Java Runtime (JRE) 7.0.60	11900	**Thursday, May 29, 2014**	

Clicking on the older version will give us the details about installing it via Chocolatey. The following are the details:

Java Runtime (JRE) 7.0.75

> This package was approved by moderator ferventcoder on 1/27/2015.

Java allows you to play online games, chat with people around the world, calculate your mortgage interest, and view images in 3D, just to name a few. It's also integral to the intranet applications and other e-business solutions that are the foundation of corporate computing.

Note

This package installs the Java version offered at https://www.java.com (currently Java 7). It also sets SPONSORS=0 (see docs).

If you want Java 8, install the jre8 package instead.

This package installs both 32 and 64-bit versions on 64-bit systems. If you only want the version specific to your OS bitness, install javaruntime-platformspecific instead.

To install Java Runtime (JRE), run the following command from the command line or from PowerShell:

```
C:\> choco install javaruntime -version 7.0.75
```

To upgrade Java Runtime (JRE), run the following command from the command line or from PowerShell:

```
C:\> choco upgrade javaruntime -version 7.0.75
```

We can see in the following screenshot that the command successfully installs Java 7.0.75:

```
C:\Users\puppet1>choco install javaruntime -version 7.0.75 -y
Chocolatey v0.9.9.7
Installing the following packages:
javaruntime
By installing you accept licenses for the packages.

javaruntime v7.0.75
 Downloading javaruntime 32 bit
    from 'http://javadl.sun.com/webapps/download/AutoDL?BundleId=101467'
 Installing javaruntime...
 Error opening file C:\Users\puppet1\AppData\LocalLow\Sun\Java\jre1.7.0_75\Java3
BillDevices.jpg
 Error: 2
 javaruntime has been installed.
 Downloading javaruntime 64 bit
    from 'http://javadl.sun.com/webapps/download/AutoDL?BundleId=101469'
 Installing javaruntime...
 Error opening file C:\Users\puppet1\AppData\LocalLow\Sun\Java\jre1.7.0_75\Java3
BillDevices.jpg
 Error: 2
 javaruntime has been installed.
 PATH environment variable does not have C:\Program Files\Java\jre7\bin in it. A
dding...
 The install of javaruntime was successful.

Chocolatey installed 1/1 package(s). 0 package(s) failed.
 See the log for details (C:\ProgramData\chocolatey\logs\chocolatey.log).

C:\Users\puppet1>
```

To update Java, we will create a new module named `chocojre`. Here is the module structure for this:

```
root@puppetmaster:/etc/puppet/modules# tree chocojre/
chocojre/
└── manifests
    └── init.pp

1 directory, 1 file
root@puppetmaster:/etc/puppet/modules#
```

Here are the details of the module:

```
# install java runtime using chocolatey
class chocojre {
  package { 'javaruntime':
    ensure   => latest,
    provider => 'chocolatey',
  }
}
```

Now, let's test this and see whether the update works as expected. First, let's be sure that the correct version was installed from Control Panel\Programs\Programs and Features in our Windows host. As we can see in the following screenshot, Chocolatey has installed both 32 and 64-bit versions of Java:

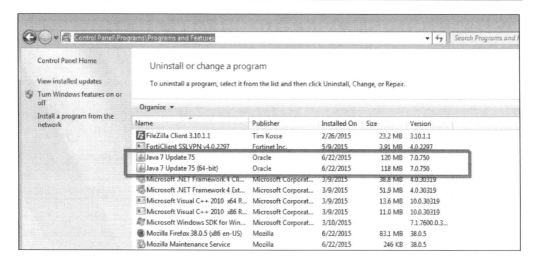

When we test run Puppet, it gives the details as shown in the following screenshot. As you can see, it has been successful:

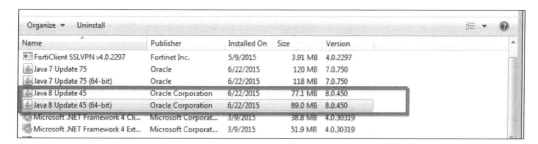

Re-checking the programs in Windows, we see that the new Java version is installed. However, there is a little problem; the old version is also there. For most software, the old version will be no more; however, this is not the case for Java.

Name	Publisher	Installed On	Size	Version	
FortiClient SSLVPN v4.0.2297	Fortinet Inc.	5/9/2015	3.91 MB	4.0.2297	
Java 7 Update 75	Oracle	6/22/2015	120 MB	7.0.750	
Java 7 Update 75 (64-bit)	Oracle	6/22/2015	118 MB	7.0.750	
Java 8 Update 45	Oracle Corporation	6/22/2015	77.1 MB	8.0.450	
Java 8 Update 45 (64-bit)	Oracle Corporation	6/22/2015	89.0 MB	8.0.450	
Microsoft .NET Framework 4 Cli...	Microsoft Corporat...	3/9/2015	38.8 MB	4.0.30319	
Microsoft .NET Framework 4 Ext...	Microsoft Corporat...	3/9/2015	51.9 MB	4.0.30319	

Using Puppet and Chocolatey to update mostly used software

We learned how to use Chocolatey to install and update a software. Now, the next step is to remove some of the burden from our shoulders. I know that there are always problems with some of the updates for certain softwares. There are always new versions and new workload to fulfill.

Here is a list of softwares that we mostly need and are frequently updated. You can, of course, create your own list:

- The Java Runtime environment
- Adobe Reader
- The Flash Player plugin
- The Flash Player plugin activex
- Firefox
- Chrome
- iTunes
- 7-Zip

After creating the list of softwares, our next step is to check `https://chocolatey.org/` and find their package names:

- **The Java Runtime environment**: `javaruntime`
- **Adobe Reader**: `adobereader`
- **The Flash Player plugin**: `flashplayerplugin`
- **The Flash Player plugin activex**: `flashplayeractivex`
- **Firefox**: `firefox`
- **Chrome**: `google-chrome-x64`
- **iTunes**: `itunes`
- **7-Zip**: `7zip`

After learning each of the package's name, you can use one module and put all of them in it, or you can create one module for each of them. It will be better if we stick to the second option. Sometimes, there are cases where you should not update a software. For example, your document management software may be using an older version of Java. Upgrading it to the newer version may just cause problems for the users. In this case, you may have to use different update policies for different softwares. Keeping the modules separate will help you to easily differentiate.

The example manifest for 7-Zip is as follows:

```
# install 7zip using chocolatey
class choco7zip {
  package { '7zip':
    ensure   => latest,
    provider => 'chocolatey',
  }
}
```

Here, by just changing the class name and package name, you can create many different modules to update different kinds of software. When you are done with these modules, you will never have to deal with the Java, Adobe, or Flash updates. This will increase your end user satisfaction, as they will not see the popups of the software updates, which they cannot complete because of missing admin rights. Also, it will help your security and you will have your updates implemented sooner. The on-time updates will patch the security problems and vulnerabilities.

If you want to keep the updates in one class, you can use the following sample class. In this class, you only need to add additional package names:

```
# update software using chocolatey
class choco7zip {

$packages = [ "javaruntime", "adobereader", " flashplayerplugin" ]

package { $packages:
    ensure   => latest,
    provider => 'chocolatey',
  }
}
```

 One more detail you need to know is that you can also use the latest option for installation. So instead of writing ensure => installed, ensure => latest will help you to install the latest version and keep it updated.

Updating the Puppet agents

One of the challenging tasks we may have is to update of the Puppet agents. Before updating the agents, ensure that the agent version is never higher than the server version. Thus, we should first start updating our server.

Updating the server

Before updating your server, ensure that you have a backup. The easiest method to update is to write the following commands. These two commands will update your Linux server and if there are any updates related to Foreman and Puppet, they will also be implemented:

```
$ sudo apt-get update
$ sudo apt-get upgrade -y
```

The following screenshot shows that there are many updates for the server:

```
puppet@puppetmaster:~$ sudo apt-get upgrade
Reading package lists... Done
Building dependency tree
Reading state information... Done
Calculating upgrade... Done
The following package was automatically installed and is no longer required:
  python-pyinotify
Use 'apt-get autoremove' to remove it.
The following packages have been kept back:
  foreman foreman-proxy linux-generic-lts-utopic
  linux-headers-generic-lts-utopic linux-image-generic-lts-utopic
  ruby-foreman-bootdisk ruby-hammer-cli ruby-hammer-cli-foreman
The following packages will be upgraded:
  apparmor binutils cpp-4.8 foreman-cli foreman-installer foreman-postgresql
  g++-4.8 gcc-4.8 gcc-4.8-base initscripts libapparmor-perl libapparmor1
  libasan0 libatomic1 libgcc-4.8-dev libgomp1 libitm1 libnuma1 libpq-dev
  libpq5 libquadmath0 libssl-dev libssl-doc libssl1.0.0 libstdc++-4.8-dev
  libstdc++6 libtsan0 linux-libc-dev openssl patch postgresql-9.3
  postgresql-client-9.3 sysv-rc sysvinit-utils wpasupplicant
35 upgraded, 0 newly installed, 0 to remove and 8 not upgraded.
Need to get 40.1 MB of archives.
After this operation, 6,337 kB of additional disk space will be used.
Do you want to continue? [Y/n]
```

After some major updates, the server may require a restart. In this case, write the following command to restart your server:

```
$ sudo reboot
```

To check the Puppet Server version, write the following command:

```
$ puppet --version
```

The following screenshot shows the output for the Puppet version. As you can see, it is 3.8.1 in the server:

```
puppet@puppetmaster:~$ puppet --version
3.8.1
puppet@puppetmaster:~$
```

Updating the agents with Chocolatey

In *Chapter 2, Installing Puppet Agents,* and in the *Installing the Puppet agent on multiple clients* section, we learned how to install the clients on multiple hosts. You can also stick to this option to send the new version of Puppet agent. However, in a corporate environment, if laptops are used, it may be hard to find every host while sending the update. Trying to find online computers and sending the updates again and again may become a burden for you. It will be much easier if Puppet also handles its agent updates.

Let's check the version in one of our hosts. We can see in the following screenshot that the current version is 3.7.4:

Now, we will upgrade it to version 3.8.1. To do this, search for `puppet` at `https://chocolatey.org/`. The following screenshot shows the `puppet` package:

Puppet 3.8.1

This package was approved by moderator gep13 on 6/1/2015.

Puppet Open Source is a flexible, customizable framework available under the Apache 2.0 license designed to help system administrators automate the many repetitive tasks they regularly perform. As a declarative, model-based approach to IT automation, it lets you define the desired state - or the "what" - of your infrastructure using the Puppet configuration language. Once these configurations are deployed, Puppet automatically installs the necessary packages and starts the related services, and then regularly enforces the desired state. In automating the mundane, Puppet frees you to work on more challenging projects with higher business impact.

Puppet Open Source is the underlying technology for Puppet Enterprise and runs on all major Linux distributions, major Unix platforms like Solaris, HP-UX, and AIX, and Microsoft Windows.

Puppet 3.7.0 is the first version that includes an 64-bit version of Puppet. Some adjustments may need to be met to upgrade to the x64 version. If you want to continue with more compatibility, please upgrade with `choco update puppet -x86`.

To install Puppet, run the following command from the command line or from PowerShell:

```
C:\> choco install puppet
```

To upgrade Puppet, run the following command from the command line or from PowerShell:

```
C:\> choco upgrade puppet
```

This is already the version we require. While testing this package, the default installation causes a restart. We do not want to disturb the users with a restart. So, we will overwrite its parameters. To do this, we need to first check the installation parameters of the puppet installation file. You can download the installation from https://downloads.puppetlabs.com/windows/. After the download, write the package name followed by /? in Command Prompt. This will show you the installation option similar to the one shown in the following screenshot:

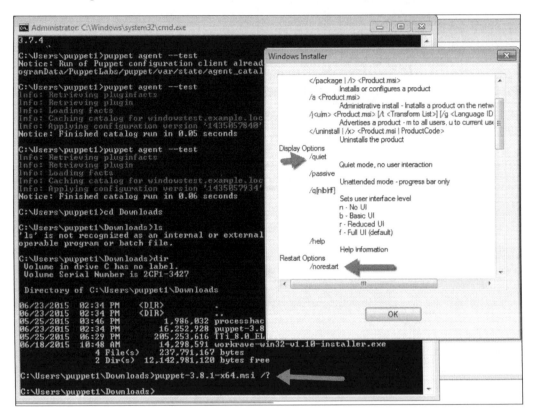

In the previous screenshot, you can see that we need two options, `/norestart` and `/quiet`, to install the agent silently and prevent a reboot. After learning these details, we are ready to continue with the manifest details.

We will create a module named `puppetagent`. The following screenshot shows the module structure:

```
puppetagent/
└── manifests
        └── init.pp

1 directory, 1 file
root@puppetmaster:/etc/puppet/modules#
```

Here are the manifest details:

```
install puppet agent using chocolatey
class puppetagent {
  package { 'puppet':
    ensure          => '3.8.1',
    install_options => ['-override', '-installArgs', '"', '/QUIET', '/NORESTART', '"'],
    provider        => 'chocolatey',
  }
}
```

In these details, we can see two more installation options:

- `-override`: This option is used to override any options that were defined

- `-installArgs`: This is used to indicate that there are new installation arguments

 Always use the version number to prevent problems. This will ensure that you are not having a version newer than your server and that you have full control over the Puppet agent versions.

After completing all the details, it is test time again. Let's see what happens when we do a test run:

```
e = ''; & import-module -name 'C:\ProgramData\chocolatey\helpers\chocolateyInsta
ller.psm1'; & 'C:\ProgramData\chocolatey\helpers\chocolateyScriptRunner.ps1' -pa
ckageScript 'C:\ProgramData\chocolatey\lib\puppet\tools\chocolateyinstall.ps1' -
installArguments '/QUIET /NORESTART' -packageParameters '' -overrideArgs"' ] exit
ed with '1'
Calling command ['"shutdown" /a']
Command ['"shutdown" /a'] exited with '1116'
Capturing package files in 'C:\ProgramData\chocolatey\lib\puppet'
 Found 'C:\ProgramData\chocolatey\lib\puppet\puppet.nupkg'
  with checksum '14656A9863E6FAF98315BE2728AB86B1'
 Found 'C:\ProgramData\chocolatey\lib\puppet\tools\chocolateyinstall.ps1'
  with checksum 'F2BA67BB123ED8D28DFBA11346179996'
Attempting to create directory "C:\ProgramData\chocolatey\.chocolatey\puppet.3.8
.1".
Attempting to delete file "C:\ProgramData\chocolatey\.chocolatey\puppet.3.8.1\.s
xs".
Attempting to delete file "C:\ProgramData\chocolatey\.chocolatey\puppet.3.8.1\.p
in".
The install of puppet was NOT successful.
Error while running 'C:\ProgramData\chocolatey\lib\puppet\tools\chocolateyinstal
l.ps1'.
 See log for details.
Moving 'C:\ProgramData\chocolatey\lib\puppet'
 to 'C:\ProgramData\chocolatey\lib-bad\puppet'

Chocolatey installed 0/1 package(s). 1 package(s) failed.
 See the log for details (C:\ProgramData\chocolatey\logs\chocolatey.log).
Failures:
 - puppet
Exiting with 1
Notice: Finished catalog run in 87.81 seconds

C:\Users\puppet1\Documents>puppet agent --version
3.8.1

C:\Users\puppet1\Documents>puppet agent --test
Info: Retrieving pluginfacts
Info: Retrieving plugin
Info: Loading facts
Info: Caching catalog for windowstest.example.local
Info: Applying configuration version '1435064128'
Notice: Finished catalog run in 1.94 seconds

C:\Users\puppet1\Documents>
```

The previous screenshot shows that it first gives an error. Although, we have put the NORESTART option, it tries to execute the shutdown /a command, which causes an error code with 1116. However, when we check the version, we can see that the update is successful. Finally, the next run gives no error as the installation is successful.

Installing Puppet 3.7.5 gives no error, However, the 3.8.1 version gives an error, which is not important. This is again the case when we may see in new open-source technologies. Putting everything together, it will be best to test any module with Chocolatey before going live.

Another problem is that sometimes, the update may not correctly run and you may need to correct it manually on the host. If your Puppet agent does not run correctly anymore, use the following command in Command Prompt to fix the agent: `choco install puppet -version 3.8.1 -force`.

Uninstalling a software

After learning the different ways of installing a software, now we will learn how to uninstall a software. At times, you may need to remove some softwares from each client. Instead of dealing with them one by one, you can use Puppet and automate the removal process. For this purpose, it is fine to use the package resource of Puppet.

As an example, we will uninstall the older versions of Java. In the following screenshot, you can see that we have both Java 7 and 8 installed. We can remove version 7:

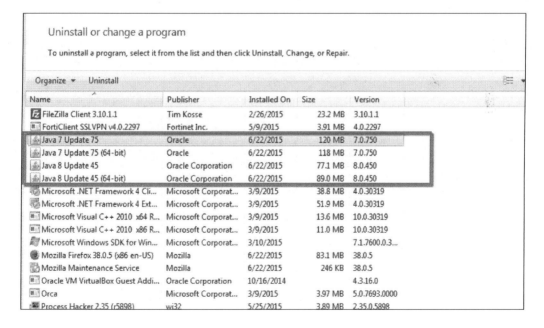

Here, we will uninstall two packages: **Java 7 Update 75** and **Java 7 Update 75 (64-bit)**. We have already created a module for Java Update: `chocojre`. Now, let's modify it so that it does not only install the latest version, but also uninstalls the older one. We will, also, require the latest version before uninstalling the previous version. There is no easy way to remove all older versions. So, we need to specify each of them manually. For uninstalling, the only change we need to add is `ensure => absent`. The following screenshot shows the modified manifest:

```
install java runtime using chocolatey
class chocojre {
  package { 'javaruntime':
    ensure   => latest,
    provider => 'chocolatey',
  }

  package { 'Java 7 Update 75':
    ensure   => absent,
    require  => Package['javaruntime'],
  }

  package { 'Java 7 Update 75 (64-bit)':
    ensure   => absent,
    require  => Package['javaruntime'],
  }
}
```

Here are the test run results:

```
C:\Users\puppet1\Documents>puppet agent --test
Info: Retrieving pluginfacts
Info: Retrieving plugin
Info: Loading facts
Info: Caching catalog for windowstest.example.local
Info: Applying configuration version '1435070160'
Notice: /Stage[main]/Chocojre/Package[Java 7 Update 75]/ensure: removed
Notice: /Stage[main]/Chocojre/Package[Java 7 Update 75 (64-bit)]/ensure: removed

Notice: Finished catalog run in 125.87 seconds

C:\Users\puppet1\Documents>_
```

At times, there are leftovers from the upgraded software; it is a good idea to remove the older versions. It will be much easier to use one module to update the same software and uninstall its older versions.

Uninstalling an older version of a software that cannot be differentiated by its name

Assume that we have a case where there are two versions of a software installed. We want to install the older version. However, we cannot differentiate them by their names because they are identical. We had this situation after upgrading Puppet. As you can see in the following screenshot, there are two different Puppet agent versions installed with the same name:

Name	Publisher	Installed On	Size	Version
Java 8 Update 45 (64-bit)	Oracle Corporation	6/22/2015	89.0 MB	8.0.450
Microsoft .NET Framework 4 Cli...	Microsoft Corporat...	3/9/2015	38.8 MB	4.0.30319
Microsoft .NET Framework 4 Ext...	Microsoft Corporat...	3/9/2015	51.9 MB	4.0.30319
Microsoft Visual C++ 2010 x64 R...	Microsoft Corporat...	3/9/2015	13.6 MB	10.0.30319
Microsoft Visual C++ 2010 x86 R...	Microsoft Corporat...	3/9/2015	11.0 MB	10.0.30319
Microsoft Windows SDK for Win...	Microsoft Corporat...	3/10/2015		7.1.7600.0.3...
Mozilla Firefox 38.0.5 (x86 en-US)	Mozilla	6/22/2015	83.1 MB	38.0.5
Mozilla Maintenance Service	Mozilla	6/22/2015	246 KB	38.0.5
Oracle VM VirtualBox Guest Addi...	Oracle Corporation	10/16/2014		4.3.16.0
Orca	Microsoft Corporat...	3/9/2015	3.97 MB	5.0.7693.0000
Process Hacker 2.35 (r5898)	wj32	5/25/2015	3.89 MB	2.35.0.5898
Puppet (64-bit)	Puppet Labs	4/21/2015	111 MB	3.7.4
Puppet (64-bit)	Puppet Labs	6/23/2015	55.8 MB	3.8.1
PuTTY version 0.63	Simon Tatham	2/26/2015	3.48 MB	0.63
Trend Micro Antivirus+	Trend Micro Inc.	5/25/2015	450 MB	8.0
Visual Studio 2012 x64 Redistribu...	AVG Technologies	5/25/2015	12.9 MB	14.0.0.1
Visual Studio 2012 x86 Redistribu...	AVG Technologies ...	5/25/2015	10.5 MB	14.0.0.1

Here, if we use `ensure => absent`, both the packages will be removed. In this case, the Puppet connection will be lost. Here, we will need a slightly advanced approach. Now, we know that the Puppet agent installation is an MSI package. Checking the registry details, we can find its uninstall string. We will run `regedit.exe` and go to the `HKLM\Software\Microsoft\Windows\CurrentVersion\Uninstall` folder. Here, we need to find Puppet version 3.7.4. The following screenshot shows the details:

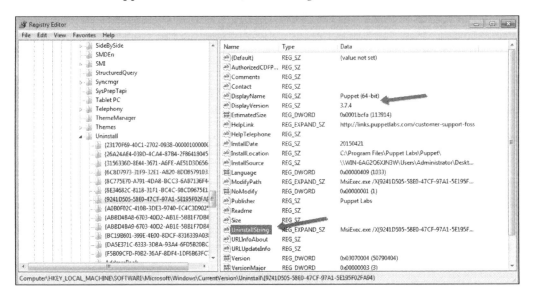

Here is the full uninstall string:

```
MsiExec.exe /X{9241D505-58E0-47CF-97A1-5E195F02FA94}
```

We will also add `/Q` so it uninstalls quietly. The new command becomes:

```
MsiExec.exe /Q /X{9241D505-58E0-47CF-97A1-5E195F02FA94}
```

When you run the uninstallation of older Puppet agents, it also breaks the newer ones. So, this is just an example to show you how to uninstall older packages. Normally, installation packages automatically remove the older version. However, it is not always the case as we see in Puppet agent and Java. As Puppet older uninstallation file breaks the newer one, never use this code in production.

We will add our uninstallation code to our `puppetagent` module. Also, we are inserting a condition that the uninstallation will only work when the Puppet agent version is 3.8.1. This will prevent the uninstallation from working, when the running version is an older one. The following screenshot shows our module with new details:

```
# install puppet agent using chocolatey
class puppetagent {
  package { 'puppet':
    ensure          => '3.8.1',
    install_options => ['-override', '-installArgs', '"', '/QUIET', '/NORESTART', '"'],
    provider        => 'chocolatey',
  }

  if $::puppetversion == '3.8.1' {
    exec { 'uninstallPuppet3.7.4':
      command       => 'MsiExec.exe /Q /X{9241D505-58E0-47CF-97A1-5E195F02FA94}',
      path          => 'C:\Windows\System32',
    }
  }
}
```

Summary

In this chapter, we learned how to install a software using the Puppet package resource. Then, we continued with the details and usage of Chocolatey. Later, we used both Puppet and Chocolatey in tandem to make our installations and updates much easier. We also checked out some of the softwares that are most used and how to always keep them updated. Finally, we learned how to update Puppet agents and uninstall a software.

We have completed our last chapter, so the book has also come to an end. If you want to learn more about Puppet, there are many more books about it. The Puppet documentation is, also, one of the places you may check out from time to time. If you have problems and need to ask questions, there are different options available such as:

- For Enterprise users, Puppet has commercial support at
  https://tickets.puppetlabs.com/secure/Dashboard.jspa

- Google groups such as puppet-users and puppet-bugs

- The #puppet IRC channel on freenode

Index

Thank you for buying
Learning Puppet for Windows Server

About Packt Publishing

Packt, pronounced 'packed', published its first book, *Mastering phpMyAdmin for Effective MySQL Management*, in April 2004, and subsequently continued to specialize in publishing highly focused books on specific technologies and solutions.

Our books and publications share the experiences of your fellow IT professionals in adapting and customizing today's systems, applications, and frameworks. Our solution-based books give you the knowledge and power to customize the software and technologies you're using to get the job done. Packt books are more specific and less general than the IT books you have seen in the past. Our unique business model allows us to bring you more focused information, giving you more of what you need to know, and less of what you don't.

Packt is a modern yet unique publishing company that focuses on producing quality, cutting-edge books for communities of developers, administrators, and newbies alike. For more information, please visit our website at www.packtpub.com.

About Packt Enterprise

In 2010, Packt launched two new brands, Packt Enterprise and Packt Open Source, in order to continue its focus on specialization. This book is part of the Packt Enterprise brand, home to books published on enterprise software – software created by major vendors, including (but not limited to) IBM, Microsoft, and Oracle, often for use in other corporations. Its titles will offer information relevant to a range of users of this software, including administrators, developers, architects, and end users.

Writing for Packt

We welcome all inquiries from people who are interested in authoring. Book proposals should be sent to author@packtpub.com. If your book idea is still at an early stage and you would like to discuss it first before writing a formal book proposal, then please contact us; one of our commissioning editors will get in touch with you.

We're not just looking for published authors; if you have strong technical skills but no writing experience, our experienced editors can help you develop a writing career, or simply get some additional reward for your expertise.

Creating Mobile Apps with Sencha Touch 2

ISBN: 978-1-84951-890-1   Paperback: 348 pages

Learn to use the Sencha Touch programming language and expand your skills by building 10 unique applications

1. Learn the Sencha Touch programming language by building real, working applications.

2. Each chapter focuses on different features and programming approaches; you can decide which is right for you.

3. Full of well-explained example code and rich with screenshots.

Sencha MVC Architecture

ISBN: 978-1-84951-888-8   Paperback: 126 pages

A practical guide for designers and developers to create scalable enterprise-class web applications in ExtJS and Sencha Touch using the Sencha MVC architecture

1. Map general MVC architecture concept to the classes in ExtJS 4.x and Sencha Touch.

2. Create a practical application in ExtJS as well as Sencha Touch using various Sencha MVC Architecture concepts and classes.

3. Dive deep into the building blocks of the Sencha MVC Architecture including the class system, loader, controller, and application.

Please check **www.PacktPub.com** for information on our titles

Learning Ext JS 4

ISBN: 978-1-84951-684-6   Paperback: 434 pages

Sencha Ext JS for a beginner

1. Learn the basics and create your first classes.

2. Handle data and understand the way it works, create powerful widgets and new components.

3. Dig into the new architecture defined by Sencha and work on real world projects.

Ext JS 4 Web Application Development Cookbook

ISBN: 978-1-84951-686-0   Paperback: 488 pages

Over 110 easy-to-follow recipes backed up with real-life examples, walking you through basic Ext JS features to advanced application design using Sencha's Ext JS

1. Learn how to build Rich Internet Applications with the latest version of the Ext JS framework in a cookbook style.

2. From creating forms to theming your interface, you will learn the building blocks for developing the perfect web application.

3. Easy to follow recipes step through practical and detailed examples which are all fully backed up with code, illustrations, and tips.

Made in the USA
Lexington, KY
24 October 2016